MW01297406

Warfleets
of
Antiquity

by Richard B. Nelson

illustrated by P. W. Norris

FIRST EDITION 1973

A Wargames Research Group Ltd publication

ISBN 978-1-326-78664-9

Published by Wargames Research Group Ltd.

Website *www.wargamesresearchgroup.net*

CONTENTS

FOREWORD TO THE 2016 EDITION

This is a reprint of the first edition of Warfleeets of Antiquity, published 40 years ago.

Since the original edition came out in 1973 there have been a number of interesting developments and new evidence, especially in underwater archaeology, both of merchant vessels and of the bronze rams fitted to warships. Three rams survive recovered from the site of the Battle of the Aegatian Islands in 241 BC. Two are Roman and bear the marks of official quality control. One is Carthaginian and is inscribed with a prayer to Baal for the success of the ship.

Equally fascinating is the working reconstruction of an Athenian Trireme (the *Olympias*) of the 5th Century BC which has allowed the testing of many operational issues and details of construction. *Olympias* is now a commissioned ship in the Greek Navy – the only modern navy to include a trireme.

An obvious major resource since the first edition of this book has been the development of the internet, which massively facilitates the speedy exploration and consideration of evidence.

Added to this edition are a set of wargames rules which were produced at the same time as the original edition. These are based on a hexagonal grid playing surface, and a subsequent development was to do away with the hexagonal playing grid and mount the ships themselves on an elongated hexagonal base. This has benefits when different sizes of ship are being used and the main rules remain otherwise valid.

Richard Nelson. June 2016

INTRODUCTION TO THE 1973 EDITION

This book has been written for readers interested in the naval history of the ancient peoples of the Mediterranean, whether as historians, ship enthusiasts, or wargamers. The period covered starts with Greek and Phoenician vessels of 800-700 BC and includes ships up to 800 AD. Where the Mediterranean peoples ventured afield into northern waters, the vessels of their enemies are also described.

The aim of the book is to fill a gap in concentrating on the practical aspects of naval warfare in antiquity, and the battles selected for description are intended to show the development of tactics and strategy, rather than illustrate the general history of the period.

The first part of the book deals with the ships themselves, with their crews, and with the problems of manning, supply, and money. The central feature of this section is a series of reconstructions of the various types of ancient vessel, making the best interpretation of the available ancient evidence.

The second part of the book is concerned with the tactics and strategy of the ancient fleets, and the main feature of this section is a series of descriptions of ancient campaigns and battles, chosen to compliment the information given in the first part of the book.

Richard Nelson. February 1973.

Sources

This list is not an exhaustive list of sources consulted, but represents a range of books on the subject which will enable the reader to follow the subject in more detail.

OARED FIGHTING SHIPS Dr. R.C. Anderson
This is a short book dealing with ship types, and covering galleys through to the 18th century.

A HISTORY OF SEAFARING based on Underwater Archaeology. Editor George F. Bass. An up to date survey of progress and discoveries in the field of underwater archaeology.

THE ANCIENT MARINERS L. Casson
A full and interestingly written book dealing with ships, crews and campaigns.

GREEK AND ROMAN NAVAL WARFARE W.L. Rodgers
Covers both ships and campaigns in considerable detail. The author was an American Admiral, and sometimes his experience overrides the ancient sources; his ship reconstructions tend to look like ironclads with the engines removed and rowing benches added. A sequel, Naval Warfare under Oars, takes his work up to the battle of Lepanto.

GREEK OARED SHIPS 900 - 322 BC. J.S. Morrison & R.J. Williams. An exhaustive account of the trireme and the ships from which it was developed.

Additional Sources

As with the first edition, there is no exhaustive source list, rather just some suggested further reading. Two additional sources which will allow readers to follow the subject in more detail are

THE AGE OF THE GALLEY. editor Robert Gardiner – part of Conway's History of the Ship series

HELLENISTIC AND ROMAN NAVAL WARS 336-31 BC

by John D Grainger published by Pen and Sword

CHRONOLOGICAL CHART

Year BC	Historical Events	Technical Developments
600		General Adoption of the Trireme as standard battleship
500	Persian Wars. Rise of Athenian Navy. Artemisium and Salamis.	Invention of Diekplus Athenian Development of manouevre tactics
400	Peloponnesian War. Battle of Pacras and Aegospotami Battles of Arginusae	Strengthened Epotides for bow to bow ramming. Invention of Quadriremes & Quinqueremes Development of Cataphract ships. Siege towers carried on paired ships.
300	Alexander Battle of Amorgos Final destruction of Athenian Navy. Battle of Salamis.	Hexeres and Hepteres invented Artillery on ships. Polyremes up to '16' built by Demetrius Pollorketes.
200	First Punic War, Rise of Roman Navy. Battles of Drepanum and Aegaces Islands	The Corvus `20' and `30' built in Egypt. Towers and artillery in general use on all cataphract ships `40' built in Egypt.
	War of Macedon, Pergamon and Rhodes Roman intervention in eastern waters.	Use of Lembi in battle by Philip of Macedon Firepots used by Rhodians
	Fall of Macedon Fall of Carthage Rise in Piracy	
100	Pirates destroyed by Pompey Caesar's campaigns in Gaul Roman Civil Wars Naulochus and Actium	Introduction of Liburnians Invention of the Harpax

PART I: THE SHIPS OF ANTIQUITY

This part of the book deals with the ships which comprised the warfleets of antiquity, how they were built and manned, and how they were maintained.

The main concern is with the ships of the Mediterranean, but the ships of the Atlantic, Channel and North Sea are also dealt-with.

The Mediterranean tradition shows the greatest diversity of shipping, with galleys ranging from the smallest sizes up to a ship over 400 feet long with a crew of 7,000. The ships of the north show a separate line of development, and some of the ships produced in northern waters were superior to their Mediterranean counterparts.

The different types of ships are described in the following section; some brief general notes apply to all the ships, however.

The surviving remains of ancient vessels show that both northern and Mediteranean ships were as a general rule built 'back to front'. In a modern ship the keel is laid, ribs are built up from it, and the hull planking is attached to the ribs.

An ancient shipwright started by making the shell of the ship with the hull planking, which was fixed plank to plank by very closely carpentered mortice and tenon joints. This 'monocoque' type of construction was then strengthened by putting ribs inside the ship to stiffen the hull frame. The frames are thus much lighter than in a modern ship.

A carvel type of construction was the rule with Mediterranean ships, with the planks of the hull edge to edge, giving a smooth exterior to the hull. Some northern ships also have a carvel construction, possibly through Roman influence, but in the north clinker hulls, with the plank edges overlapping each other, are the rule.

Merchant vessels in the Mediterranean were protected from teredo worm etc. by lead sheets covering the area of hull below the water line. It is likely that warships were not so protected, but since warships were regularly hauled ashore and beached, and spent the winter out of the water and under cover, the need was not so great. Warships had a life of about 20/25 years, but the record is held by a 16, the flagship of the Macedonian fleet, which was still capable of being sailed in triumph up the Tiber by the Romans over 100 years after it was first launched.

Despite the careful carpentering, ships were in some cases built with considerable speed, and entire fleets were ready within months of the initial order to start construction. This is particularly so of the Romans.

The record time recorded is 45 days from the date the order to start felling timber was given.

SHIP PERFORMANCE

It is difficult to give figures for the actual performance of ancient warships, because of the wide number of variable factors involved.

The ships used in the Mediterranean carried both oars and sails, although it was invariable to leave the main mast and sail behind when going into action. Since the ships did not have keels, the sail was only useful when the wind was favourable; indeed over a long voyage it was reckoned that a fleet made better time under oars, not sail, despite the strain on the rowers.

On a long voyage it was in any case usual, whether under oars or sail, to stop at night and anchor or beach; warships often stopped in the middle of the day to allow the crews to cook dinner ashore. Whether using oars or sail, therefore, fleets made about 30 miles per day (average speed about 3-4 knots) and either coasted or hopped from island to island. On occasion fleets did cross open sea. Ptolemy took 350 ships from Egypt to Cyprus (200 miles) in 306 BC, and the Romans set off from Panormus in Sicily direct to Rome in 253 BC (typically losing 150 ships in a storm on the way).

Under battle conditions, the main factor affecting performance was the standard of-rowing; far more than ship design. Of course ship designs varied, and there were light and heavy variants of the various types of warship, but in general warship designs were standard from fleet to fleet. The dress and equipment of the crew was often the only indication of nationality. Prizes were usually welcome reinforcements.

Nevertheless, light ships were faster than heavy, and fleets relying on manouevre built light as policy. But a light ship with poor rowers was inferior to a heavy ship with good rowers.

Because there was a limit to the rowers stamina, there were three different speeds for an ancient warship.

Maximum speed was attained with all the rowers exerting their full power, and could be maintained only for about 20 minutes.

Fast cruise involved all the rowers at an easy stroke, and could be maintained for perhaps 3 hours. A battle would be fought at speeds between maximum and fast cruise.

Slow cruise was the usual method of rowing on a long journey, and involved only some of the rowers. In a trireme one bank was normally manned and the other two banks were resting at this speed.

The galleys of 3 centuries ago did not attain speeds much in excess of 7 knots. Ships in antiquity were probably faster, being lighter in build. Ancient rowers, who were free men, were also more willing, and in better physical condition, than the prisoners of war and convicts who propelled the ships of later times.

Under oars, then, ancient galleys could attain up to 9 knots at maximum speed, 4-5 knots at fast cruise, and 3 knots at slow cruise.

In attaining these speeds, the training and experience of the rowers was important. Experienced oarsmen consistently outrowed inexperienced, and were in demand accordingly. Equally important was crew training. It took a while for a crew to work together efficiently, and constant practice was necessary to maintain performance. When on campaign a fleet normally spent the day in exercises if opportunity offered.

Ships often lacked full crews. At one stage in the Peloponnesian war one Athenian fleet was down to less than 70% crews on average, and the Romans besieging Lilybaeum in 249 BC. lost so many rowers in the siege works that a draft of 10,000 was needed before the fleet could again take the sea.

More important than the design of a ship was the amount of gear it was carrying, in determining performance. The main mast and sail were always left ashore before battle, and heavy appliances like the corvus were a considerable handicap. Warships normally had only about 3 days stores, but if caught in passage when loaded with stores for a campaign they were at a big disadvantage.

If ships were equipped with towers, these were usually prefabricated and would be jettisoned by a losing fleet to get more speed to escape.

There was little to chose between different ancient warships in terms of speed. The 3 and 4 were the fastest; larger ships had the advantage of large numbers of marines. Smaller vessels did not have the same speed as bigger, nor, lacking the reserves of rowers, the same endurance, but made up for this by cheapness and manouevrability.

Speeds attained under sail were normally not high, and the sail was only of use if the wind was favourable. The primary use of the sail was to rest the rowers, and 6/7 knots is probably a reasonable speed for a warship under sail, slightly faster than a merchant vessel. This is only half the speed attained by modern sailing vessels.

Vessels designed to operate under oars and sail, the 1 ½ and 2 ½ may have attained up to 10 knots or more.

Turning circles and manouevrability were very variable, although obviously governed by vessels size, because oars as well as the efficient steering oars were used in the turn, and the efficiency of the crew was thus again paramount.

Even using the steering oars alone, vessels like the 3 and 4 were quite handy, despite their length. At a battle speed the turning circle may have been 250ft. diameter, taking approx. 1 minute to do the 360°.

A vessel would also in battle be likely to spend a considerable time backing water, usually as a means of avoiding outflanking, and to keep the ram pointed towards the enemy.

THE SAILS OF ANCIENT SHIPS

It used to be believed that the square rig was the only rig known to antiquity, and that the lateen and other fore and aft sails were the invention of later generations.

It is certainly true that the normal sail plan for most ships was one square sail on a single mast. On early warships and on some merchant vessels this is a particularly long and narrow sail; on other merchant ships the sail is much squarer.

However by the 5th century BC warships were carrying two square sails. One was the mainsail, the second was a smaller foresail (called the boat sail) carried on an auxiliary mast like a bowsprit. Both masts could be easily struck, and were usually struck for battle, when the main mast and sail would be left ashore if possible.

The first illustration (on the page opposite) shows the general appearance of the sails carried by warships in Greek times; on Roman ships the sails were somewhat squarer.

There is also evidence that by 450 BC merchant ships with two masts corresponding to the warship's two masts were in existence in the western Mediterranean. The typical rig of the Roman merchantman, big mainsail and smaller artemon, is thus found very early in the Classical period.

On later Roman representations Merchant ships are shown with up to three masts, all square rigged, but still with one mainsail only per mast. The only exception to the one sail: one mast rule is that a small triangular sail is usually carried on Roman ships above the main yard and may be earlier than the Roman period.

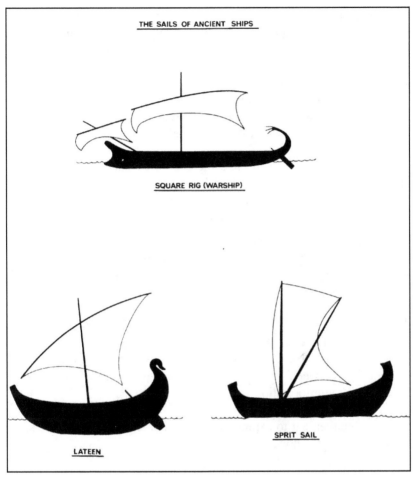

THE SAILS OF ANCIENT SHIPS

SQUARE RIG (WARSHIP)

SPRIT SAIL

LATEEN

Rigging differed from modern rigging chiefly in that shrouds were not used to support masts which were so frequently raised and lowered. The only lateral support for warship masts was that supplied by a double forestay; the halyards also provided some degree of lateral support. Shrouds are however found on later Roman merchantmen. Reefing sails was done from deck level. A number of lines ran down the face of the sail through bronze rings to the foot of the sail, and by hauling on these lines the foot of the sail would be raised, reducing its area.

It is now known that the square sail was not the only sail known in antiquity. Representations of sails very close to the lateen have been found dating from the second century AD on small vessels, so this sail is a very much older type than had been believed.

A more common type of fore and aft sail from antiquity is the sprit sail, previously thought to have been a Dutch invention in the 15th century AD. The third illustration shows this type of sail.

In the sprit sail one edge of the sail is secured to the mast and the peak of the sail is supported by a spar running diagonally from the base of the mast. Sometimes one spritsail was used; sometimes two, one each side of the mast, were employed to run before the wind.

The sprit sail was used on large merchantmen instead of the square rig; a reduced crew was required but there was some loss of speed before the wind. It is possible that ships were rigged with the spritsail or some other fore and aft rig by the time of Alexander.

Northern barbarians appear to have used only the square rig, but the Byzantines used the lateen extensively, and the usual rig for dromons was two (perhaps three on large ships) masts, each with one lateen sail. Such sails were not struck before battle but were kept furled.

THE COST OF NAVAL WARFARE

It is very difficult to relate the costs of things in ancient times to modern values. Nevertheless, we can give some idea of the relationship between the various costs and wages in ancient times, based upon the information which is available to us.

It will be convenient to express all costs in drachmae. The conversion table for Athenian money is:

6 obols	1 drachma
100 drachmae	1 mina
60 minae	1 talent

At the time of the Peloponnesian War, the daily rate of pay for a rower was 3 obols, or 0.5 drachma. The cost of the Trierarchy, in other words the cost to the Trierarch of keeping one trireme in good order for one year, was 40-60 minae, or 4,000 - 6,000 drachmae. At the time of the Persian Wars, the cost of a new trireme was 1 talent, or 6,000 drachmae.

It is at once clear that the cost of building a trireme is almost the same as the cost of maintaining it for one year; however there was some degree of inflation between the Persian wars and the Peloponnesian, and the cost of one talent did not probably include the cost of fitting out the ship or equipping it.

The cost of one new trireme at the time of the Peloponnesian war is thus estimated at 2 talents or 12,000 drachmae, and the cost of maintenance at between 30% and 50% of this figure. We know that a trireme needed to carry 50% spare oars to allow for breakage during the season; it would appear that the other costs are in proportion, which is what we might expect from a lightly built galley on war service.

The cost of paying the crew was borne by the state, not the Trierarch. Taking the trireme crew at a round figure of 200, the cost of wages for one month works out at 3,000 drachmae; for a season's commission of up to 8 months, 24,000 drachmae, or twice the cost of a new trireme and 4 to 6 times the cost of the trierarchy. The cost of food for the crew need not be taken in to account; in the Athenian fleet they were expected to buy their own, and an admiral had to base his ships therefore near a convenient market.

For larger ships in the Hellenistic period with a bigger crew, the pay of the crew will have formed an even greater proportion of the fleet costs.

As an extremely general rule, therefore, we may suggest that the total cost of an ancient fleet was about 25% higher than the cost of the crew's pay.

We are informed that the Rhodians at a later period chartered out some triremes at 10,000 drachmae per month; costs and wages were perhaps double what they were in the Peloponnesian war, so the price will have included 6,000 drachmae wages and 1,500 drachmae for the ships and their upkeep, leaving a 30% profit, which we might have expected from so commercially minded a people.

The cost of ships in the Roman fleets was probably similar to that in Hellenistic times, about twice the Peloponnesian War figure. A seaman in a Roman Imperial fleet probably received 100 denarii, equivalent to 330 drachmae, or about 1 drachma per day.

In more modern times, the cost of building a wooden ship corresponded to the formula; cost per ton equals 1 day's pay for a shipwright times 120.

Taking a trireme at 50 tons and a shipwright's pay at 1 drachma, this gives a figure of 6,000 drachmae, equal to the recorded figure of 1 talent.

This is too low, but as the mortice and tenon mode of building probably took more time than modern methods, the figure of 120 probably needs adjusting upwards. In Byzantine times the building cost of a ship was about 45 solidi per ton, or equal to a labourer's wage for a year.

Taking a shipwright as earning twice a labourer's wage, this gives a multiplier for the formula of 180 for Byzantine times, when the mortice and tenon construction was already being modified and simplified.

A figure of 200-220 for classical times gives confirmation of the cost of the trireme already arrived at.

MAINTENANCE & DOCKYARD FACILITIES

Although the warships and merchant vessels of the Mediterranean and North were originally designed for beaching, and no formal harbours existed, the main commercial and naval powers eventually maintained proper ports for both merchant and war fleets.

Merchant fleets used ports very similar to those in use today, mooring alongside quays of stone which were protected either by natural features or by moles. Alternatively artificial harbours were created by excavating enclosed docks, as at Carthage and Rome.

The warship required somewhat different facilities. Merchant ships stayed in the water continually, and were protected by lead sheeting against marine creatures. The lighter warships were not so protected, and for preservation had to be regularly hauled out of the water for drying. On campaign ships were beached at night. Over the winter, when they were laid up, they had to be kept preserved from the elements.

The most characteristic feature of an ancient naval base was therefore lines of ship sheds, long narrow structures covering and enclosing permanent slipways up which ships could be hauled clear of the water.

Typical shipsheds are illustrated, based on excavated examples at Athens, where there were over 350 sheds to accommodate the warships. The length and distance between the surviving slipways gives us maximum dimensions for the ships that they could accommodate.

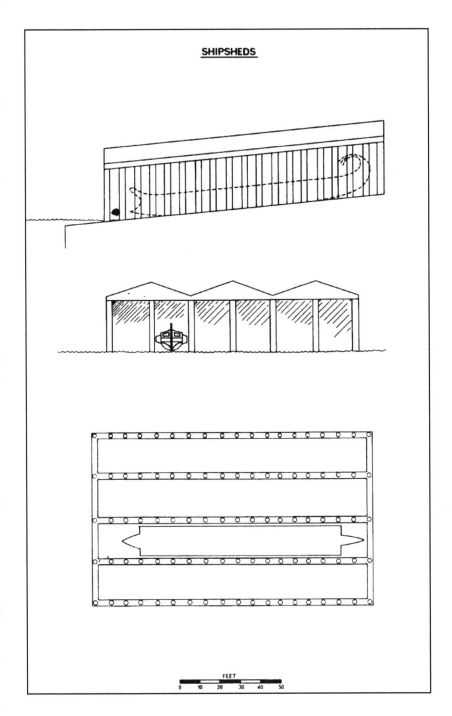

SHIPSHEDS

FEET
0   10   20   30   40   50

Shipsheds were often highly decorated; at Carthage the military harbour was an architectural showpiece, with columns at the waters edge giving the effect of a huge colonnade. The harbour was circular in form, with sheds all the way round the edge, and with a circular island in the centre, again with shipsheds reaching down to the water, and the naval Headquarters in the centre of the island. At Athens the two smaller harbours on the south side of Piraeus were exclusively military; the bigger harbour on the north side of the peninsula was mainly commercial, but also contained shipsheds.

The Imperial Roman fleets each had a home base, which often gave its name to the fleet (e.g. Ravenna & Misenum). The Classis Britannica however had its home base at Boulogne, to ensure access to Britain from the continent was always available.

It is clear from surviving records that naval powers kept detailed records of stores, and were concerned to maintain supplies of essential materials. Several treaties of the Athenians with smaller powers survive, guaranteeing the supply of timber or in one case Ruddle or red ochre, one of the uses of which was as an ingredient in paint.

A remarkably modern degree of security consciousness often surrounded naval bases; not so much because of secrecy, but because of the opportunity for sabotage presented by so much inflammable material.

It was thought one of the more perfidious acts of Philip V of Macedon that he sent an emissary (one Heracleides) to Rhodes, who took advantage of his friendly reception to set fire to part of the Dockyard and disappear.

THE SHIPS

This section gives scale reconstructions of the major ship types of antiquity, in chronological order.

The reconstructions are based upon the best surviving ancient evidence, but it must be appreciated that many points of major detail remain disputed. All the vessels shown, however, with the exception of the 40 of Ptolemy IV and the Veneti ship, are based at least in part on surviving remains or ancient representations, and for the 40 most of the major dimensions have been recorded because the ship was unique.

In general, masts and sails have not been shown, except where they were the main means of propulsion. We do not even know how many masts the big Hellenistic polyremes had. A separate section on sails is given, as much of the evidence applies in general to the whole range of ships.

Sources are briefly indicated, but this book is not the place for a detailed argument over the interpretation of the evidence.

Figures for the crews of the various ships are given; except where stated these are maxima, and different navies with different tactical ideas varied the number of marines very considerably.

The naming of different types of ships in general follows common usage; thus the Athenian 3 is called a trireme, not a trieres, and a Rhodian 4 is called a quadrireme, not a tetreres.

With greatly varying sizes of the ships shown, it has not been possible to reproduce all the drawings to a constant scale, but a scale of feet is given for each set of drawings, to facilitate comparison.

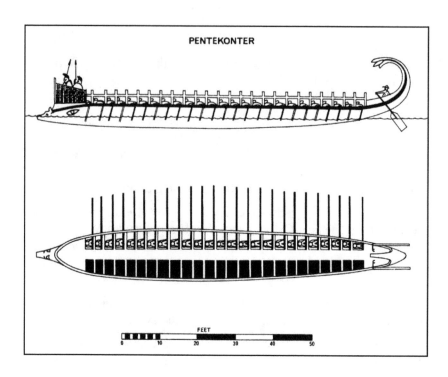

PENTEKONTER

FEET

GREEK TRIAKONTER & PENTEKONTER

The earliest Greek galleys of which we have knowledge are the Triakonter and Pentekonter, propelled by 30 and 50 oars respectively, 15 and 25 per side.

The Pentekonter was the standard warship before the Trireme was introduced, and limited numbers remained with fleets after that date to act as scouts and despatch boats.

Like all galleys, a single mast and sail were carried for cruising, but all fighting was done under oars and the mast and sail left behind if possible before going into action.

Both vessels already display the main constructional features of the Greek galley. There are three main longitudinal timbers. One forms the keel, and the two others the gunwales. The gunwales are brought down to join the keel and form the ram, and all three timbers sweep up at the stern and join together to form the characteristic scorpions tail. The longitudinal timbers are joined by ribs at intervals of about 3 ft, and these ribs are carried above the level of the gunwales. The oars are attached to these ribs by leather thongs, or to separate single thole pins in the gunwale.

The rowers sit in the open. It is probable that their benches were carried across the ship from side to side, and supported a central gangway from bow to stern.

The ships have no rudder, but are steered by two steering oars; the helmsman sits in the stern, and controls the oars by short handles at right angles to the oar.

There is a small foredeck for marines protected by a wicker screen, above the ram of bronze, shaped like the head of an animal. However at this period of history ram tactics were not yet developed, and battles were mainly settled by boarding.

Pentekonter details:

length: 100ft. beam: 14ft. draft: 2.5 ft.

rowers: 50, each with one oar

others: 10 approx.
Total: 60

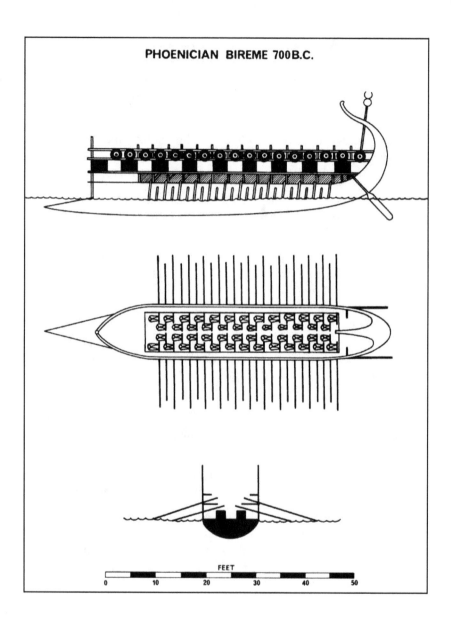

PHOENICIAN BIREME 700 B.C.

FEET

0   10   20   30   40   50

PHOENICIAN BIREME 700 B.C.

This reconstruction is based upon well known sculptures from Nineveh.

The ship has the same number of rowers as the pentekonter, but a greater power per foot of length because they are disposed on two levels. Since the upper rowers are visible in the representation, it is inferred that they sat outboard of the lower oarsmen. A possible oar arrangement is illustrated.

A single mast and sail are carried, and are stowed along the centre line when not in use. There is a large ram, but the extensive screening of the upperworks indicates reliance on boarding and the carrying of large numbers of archers. Ram tactics were not developed at this time.

The formation of the upperworks suggests how this vessel was developed into the trireme. The frames are carried well above the level of the gunwales and the oars, as on the pentekonter, About 2ft. above the gunwale a wicker screen, painted in particoloured squares, is fixed, and above that the frames are open, but carry round shields.

There are evidently gangways along each side of the ship behind the screens, and decks at bow and stern on the level of the gangways.

This ship could be lengthened to accommodate more rowers; double the number here could be carried without the ship being longer than the pentekonter. A larger ship could carry more marines and would be preferred to the 50 rower vessel shown.

Such an increase in length would need an increase in beam to keep the ratio about 8 : 1, but the curvature of the ships side would tend to pinch in the rowers at the ends of the vessel.

Two developments would overcome this problem, and again increase the oarpower of the ship. First, by making the sides of the ship at oarlevel straight, the rowers would not be pinched in;

Second, by turning the gangways above the two levels of existing rowers into a rectangular planform frame, and putting rowers instead of marines on it, a 50% increase in oarsmen could be accommodated. Such a ship would be a trireme, of which the developed version follows.

Phoenician Bireme Data

Dimensions		Crew	
length:	70 ft.	rowers	50 (50 oars)
beam:	11 ft.	marines	25
draught:	3ft.	sailors etc.	10

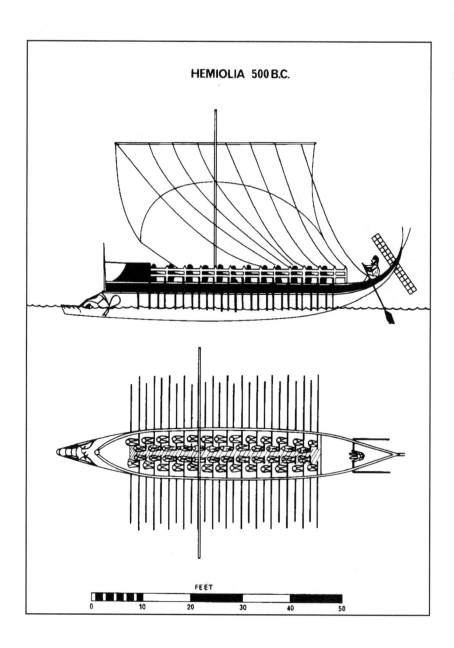

HEMIOLIA 500 B.C.

FEET

0   10   20   30   40   50

HEMIOLIA 500 B.C.

This vessel, whose name means one-and-a-half, was the usual Pirate vessel. Speed being essential, it is designed to operate under oars and sail, as even a slow merchantman under sail, if given a reasonable start, could not be overtaken by a galley before the rowers became tired.

The ship is very similar to a two banked pentekonter, and has the usual warship features. When attacking a merchant ship, the hemiola would approach under oars and sail, possible as fast as 10 knots, or twice the best speed of the merchantman. On nearing the prey, the oarsmen in the upper bank abaft the mast would ship their oars, and strike the mast and sail, leaving the final manouevre and approach to be done under 1½ banks, hence the name hemiola. The spare oarsmen meantime would form a useful reinforcement to the boarding party, and could also act as prize crew.

Although the hemiolia was very fast with the wind behind it, it was not suitable for battle use by regular navies. A ship with the sail up was at a distinct disadvantage where fast manouevre through 360° was required, and with the sail down the hemiola was no different from a pentekonter.

The speed of the hemiola was however very useful in escaping from warships; pirates with the wind behind them could outrun any warship under oars alone, and if the warship tried to pursue under oars and sail the pirates had only to let the warship come up close, then strike their own sail and row off directly into the wind. Since the warship could not strike its own mast with the same speed, the pirates would evade capture.

The Rhodian navy, however, devised a successful pirate catcher, the triemiolia or 2½. This was a trireme, modified to operate under oars and sail exactly like the hemiolia, just as fast, and with a crew of 200 instead of the 60 or so of the pirate craft. It could thus catch the hemiola, and then easily overwhelm it by boarding.

The sail plan of the hemiola is similar to other ships of the period. Note the lines from the top of the yard. These led down the face of the sail through rings sewn to it to the sail foot, and were used for reefing the sail. All sail control was done from deck level.

The structure behind the helmsman is the ladder used by the crew as a gangway when the vessel was beached.

Hemiola data
length: 70 ft. beam: 10 ft. draft: 2.5 ft.
Crew rowers: 52, each with one oar, 14 of whom form the mast strike party. others: 10 approx.

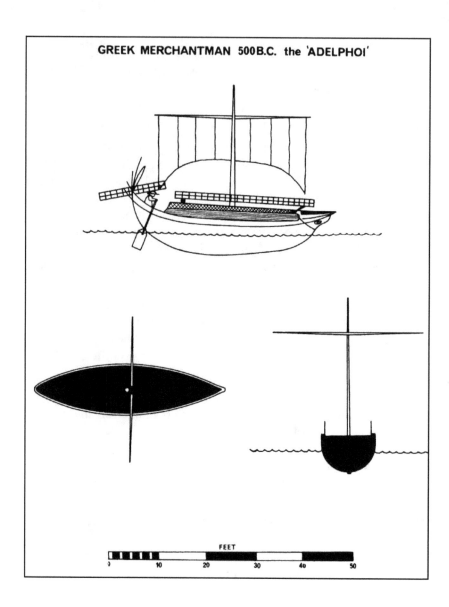

GREEK MERCHANTMAN 500B.C. the 'ADELPHOI'

FEET
0   10   20   30   40   50

GREEK MERCHANTMAN 500 B.C. THE `ADELPHOI'

This is a typical small merchant vessel, a round ship as opposed to the long warships, propelled by a single square sail instead of by oars.

The ship has a capacity of about 40 tons, and a single hold. It is completely decked. There is a wicker screen along the side of the ship, and the helmsman, as usual, sits in the stern controlling double steering oars.

The structure above the wicker screen appears to be a ladder for the crew to ascend the mast, as there were no shrouds.

Merchant ships could carry sweeps, but using oars for normal commercial purposes was not usual. To employ 20 rowers at this period for the sailing season might have cost 1500-2000 drachmae, a sum well beyond the means of the small shipowners who usually had one vessel and sailed with it. Nevertheless, hybrid oared merchantmen are found, and there were probably used as military transports primarily.

This ship has a single square sail; recent evidence suggests that 2 masts were already known in the western Mediterranean at this period, and fore and aft sails within 200 years.

The vessel illustrated is fairly small; ships double the length were quite usual, and a vessel of 250 tons capacity was not unique at the period of the Peloponnesian War.

The name Adelphoi (the Two Brothers) is recorded as an Ancient Merchant ship name.

Greek Merchantman data

Dimensions

Length 40 ft. Beam 11 ft. Draft 6 ft.

Crew   6/7 including Owner/Master.

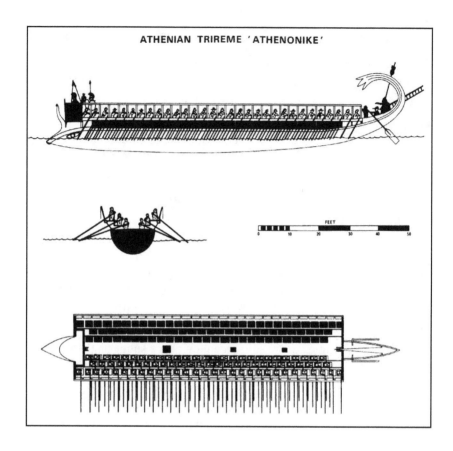

ATHENIAN TRIREME 'ATHENONIKE'

ATHENIAN TRIREME 430 B.C.   'ATHENONIKE'

This is the Trireme developed out of the Phoenician Bireme in its classical form. The sides of the vessel are open, permitting all three levels of rowers to be seen. The uppermost rowers, called thranites, of whom there are 31 per side, have their thole pins on an outrigger (parekseiresia) rectangular in plan, supported on the frames of the ship.

The lowest rowers (thalamites) have their thole pins on the curved gunwales of the vessel; there are 27 thalamites per side and 27 zeugites sitting between them and the thranites. The zeugites thole pins are supported on a timber halfway between gunwale and parekseiresia. There are thus a total of 170 rowers, each with one oar about 14ft. long. All the rowers were free men, as usual in antiquity, and the rate of pay in 430 B.C. was half a drachma per day, or 3 obols. By the end of the Peloponnesian War this had risen to 4 obols, and the rate was about 1 drachma in Hellenistic times.

ATHENIAN TRIREME 430 B.C.   'ATHENONIKE'

The usual galley features, upcurved stern, double steering oar, and ram bow, are found. The ram is described as triembolon and had three points, one above the other, rather than the animal's head or simple point of earlier times. Later rams were developed (at least in art) into tridents and similar decorative forms. Above the ram is a hornlike feature, which was carried from this time by all ships relying on ramming, The object was to push the rammed enemy away, and prevent the ram going in too far. If this happened, the ramming ship was stuck to a sinking enemy, vulnerable to irate enemy marines, or to being rammed by another enemy vessel.

The frames are carried above the level of the parekseiresia to support leather screens, which were rigged in battle as a defence against missiles. These screens were called parablemata.

The usual mast and single square sail were carried, but now an auxiliary boat sail is carried. This latter sail, probably looking like the bowsprit artemon sail carried by Roman ships, was left on board in battle and was used for escape from a defeat.

The Athenians had 14 marines (10 hoplites and 4 archers) in naval battles; when used in support of land operations they carried 20 hoplites. Greek states who relied on boarding had up to 40 marines.

It was usual for missilemen to throw sitting down, which tells us something about the general stability of the ship. The 4 Athenian archers were probably at the ends of the parekseiresia. 'Athenonike', a composite word formed from Athene or Athens and Victory, was a favourite ship name and was revived by the Romans for ships of the Imperial fleet.

Trireme Data

Dimensions		Crew	
length:	120 ft.	rowers:	170
beam:	18 ft. over outriggers	sailors etc.	20
	13ft. hull max.	marines:	14
draught: 3 ft.		fuller details are given in the section on crews.	

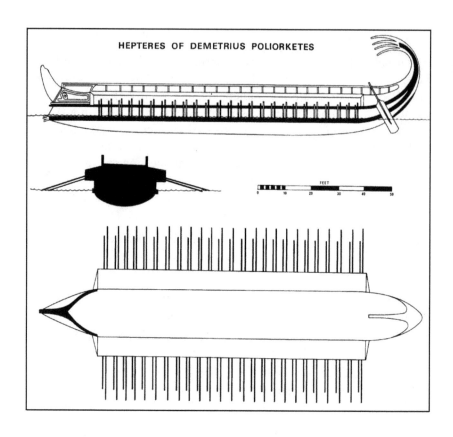

HEPTERES OF DEMETRIUS POLIORKETES

FEET
0 10 20 30 40 50

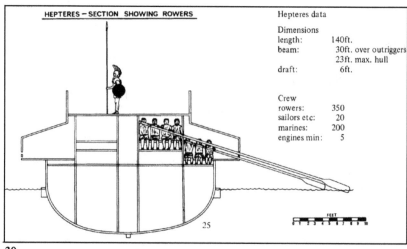

HEPTERES – SECTION SHOWING ROWERS

Hepteres data

Dimensions
length: 140ft.
beam: 30ft. over outriggers
               23ft. max. hull
draft: 6ft.

Crew
rowers: 350
sailors etc: 20
marines: 200
engines min: 5

25

FEET
0 1 2 3 4 5 6 7 8 9 10

HEPTERES OF DEMETRIUS POLIORKETES 306 B.C. 'ANTIGONIS'

In the years between 400 and 390 B.C. new types of vessel were developed in Sicilian waters; the quadrireme and quinquereme, with respectively 4 and 5 rowers where the trireme had 3. Such vessels probably differed little from the trireme (and at Athens used the same size slipways), but represented a new principle in that more than 1 man manned each oar. By 322 B.C. the fleet of Athens was largely composed of quadriremes, and the trireme was superseded as the standard battleship. In the fleets of Alexander's Successors the quadrireme and quinquereme were standard.

These vessels were cataphract; that is to say there was a complete deck for marines above the rowers, who were now entirely hidden, and the parekseiresia took the form of an enclosed box on the ship's side. The complete deck was partly an answer to the tactical requirements of the Successors, but the use of multiple rowers on an oar meant that such a deck need not be relatively so high as on a trireme. When in 306 B.C. Demetrius Poliorketes took Cyprus from Ptolemy of Egypt, he had no less than seven Hepteres or 7s, built in Phoenicia, and these vessels formed the spearhead of his victorious left wing at the battle of Salamis.

The reconstruction of the 7 is based upon the coin which Demetrius issued after his victory, showing his flagship. The sectional drawing shows the arrangement of the rowers, with 4 men on one oar and 3 men on the second shorter oar. Although the rowers are at different levels their oars have their thole pins at approximately the same height on the ships side. A long timber wale runs along the vessel's side at the waterline; this was probably designed as a defence against ramming, and it is known that Roman ships 300 years later were protected in this fashion.

It is certain that Demetrius mounted artillery on his ships. Such engines were purely antipersonnel weapons, not ship killers, and included both dart and stone throwers, and were carried in later fleets by all cataphract vessels. Even in the Rhodian navy, which was a `ram' rather than `board' fleet, catapultist was a regular crew grading. The portable towers used in later times were not however carried at this period, although modified vessels carried big towers for siege operations.

The name Antigonis is a natural one for Demetrius to give to one of his vessels, being the female form of Antigonus, his father's name. Ships were female, and while it was possible to name a ship after some notable person, the female version of the name had to be used.

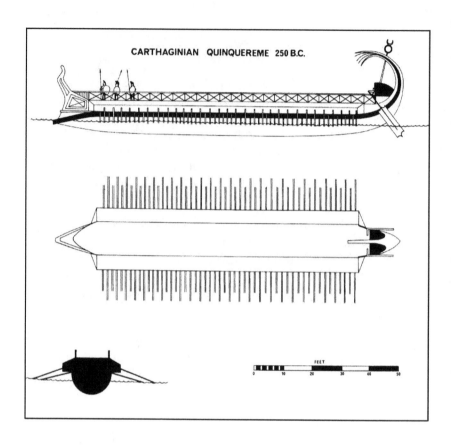

CARTHAGINIAN QUINQUEREME 250 B.C.

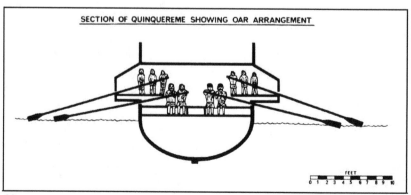

SECTION OF QUINQUEREME SHOWING OAR ARRANGEMENT

CARTHAGINIAN QUINQUEREME 250 B.C.

Although invented before the Hepteres, the quinquereme is taken out of chronological order, as the vessel illustrated is a Carthaginian example of the First Punic War.

The reconstruction is based upon Punic coins, and shows oars at two levels, with respectively 3 and 2 rowers per oar. There are 60 oars per side, corresponding with the recorded number of rowers (300). Roman vessels of this type, which were copies of the Carthaginian, carried up to 120 marines, of whom 40 were a permanent guard of proletarii assigned to the ship, and 80 a draft of legionaries (perhaps one century) put on board for an actual battle. The vessel shown here has the disc and crescent ensign carried by all Punic and Phoenician warships; with a change of insignia it could be a Roman ship.

Despite their large crews, Roman quinqueremes were by 200 B.C. very lightly constructed. It was necessary to put the oars in the water to steady the ship to throw grapnels. The Consul Marcellus escaped across a boom in Syracuse harbour by moving all his marines to the stern of his ship, thus bringing the bows out of the water, and rowing full ahead. With the ship well on top of the boom, the marines moved into the bows, depressing the fore part of the ship, and inducing it to slide forward over the obstacle!

The quinquereme is a typical Cataphract ship, and the Quadrireme, which was the standard ship of the Rhodian fleet in particular, must have been very similar externally, but with a slightly reduced beam, and a 2 plus 2 arrangement of rowers as opposed to the 3 plus 2 of the quinquereme.

Quinqueremes were built in light and heavy versions, and there was probably some variation in oar arrangements as well, with some heavier vessels having 30 oars per side and 5 men per oar.

Quinquereme data

Dimensions
length: 120 ft.
beam: 20 ft. over parekseiresia
14 ft. hull
draft: 4 ft.

Crew
rowers: 300
sailors etc: 20
marines 75 approx.

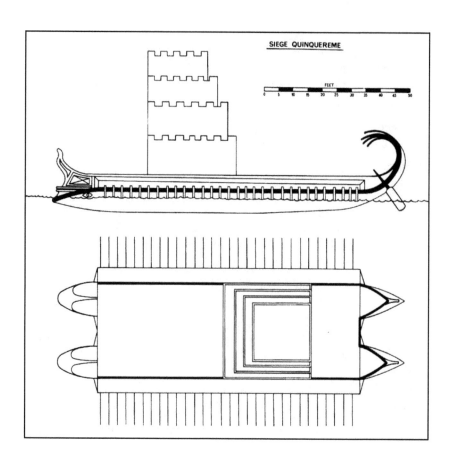

SIEGE QUINQUEREME

MODIFIED QUINQUEREME (SIEGE)

The potentialities of warships and merchant vessels in siege operations was well recognised by the ancients, and many ingenious modifications exploited the ability of ships to get large structures or heavy weights up to the walls of coastal cities.

The commonest type of modification was to secure two vessels together to form a stable platform.

The illustration shows two cataphract quinqueremes which have been so joined. The deck railings have been removed and a large joint deck added, on which a siege tower has been erected. The tower has the common Hellenistic form of diminishing stories, and the lower stories at least would house forward firing stone throwing engines.

One bank of rowers has been deleted, as only a restricted movement is necessary.

Towers were carried in this way by the Macedonians by 350 B.C., and in later years the heaviest engines were also carried by warships, often behind screens to protect the crew from enemy counterfire.

Lashing two ships together in this way probably suggested the catamaran construction of Ptolemy's 40.

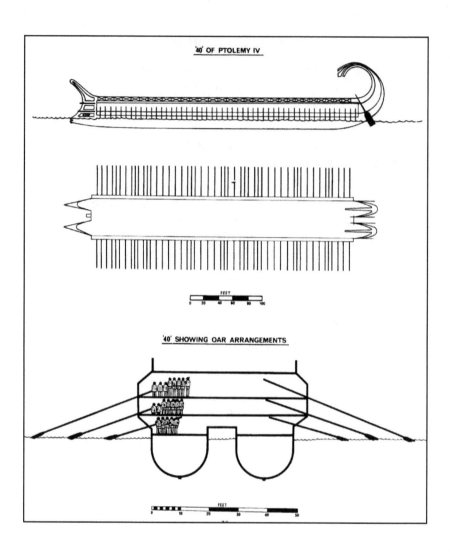

'40' OF PTOLEMY IV

FEET
0 20 40 60 80 100

'40' SHOWING OAR ARRANGEMENTS

FEET
0 10 20 30 40 50

THE 40   215 B.C.

In the last part of the 3rd Century B.C. Ptolemy IV of Egypt, surnamed Philopater, had constructed the largest galley known to Antiquity. This is the famous 40.

Because of its unique size, many of the dimensions of this vessel have been recorded, as well as details of the construction. The reconstruction shows a catamaran type of hull; this is the logical interpretation of her having had 2 bows, 2 sterns, and 4 steering oars. Lashing ships together in pairs was a well known operation and the construction of a double hull was no great step, therefore.

The longest oars are called 'thranite', suggesting that the oars were carried on 3 levels, with 3 separate decks for the rowers. There are literary references to earlier ships having 3 decks. A total of 4,000 rowers is given, suggesting 50 sets of oars a side. Manned on a push/pull system, with 7 feet between oars, this takes up the reasonable amount of 350ft. out of the 429ft. length. The rowing system suggested is 8 plus 8 thranite, 7 plus 7 zeugite, and 5 plus 5 thalamite oarsmen.

The 40 is normally said to have been unseaworthy because of her great length, but with the ancient type of monocoque construction the length of the keel timber (the limit in more modern times) will not have applied. The 40's impracticability is rather that like all ancient galleys, the crew were not intended to live on the ship, which would normally berth at night. Embarking and disembarking 7000 men would take hours out of every day, and when they were installed in the ship, coordinating the efforts of 4000 rowers on 3 decks would present a formidable communication problem. Finally, her huge crew could equally man 12 quinqueremes representing a much more serviceable contribution to the fleet.

Under the circumstances, therefore, the 40 remains a `toy' of an ostentatious Hellenistic monarch, but it shows what the ancients were capable of producing.

40 data

Dimensions		Crew	
length:	429 ft.	rowers:	4000
beam:	58ft. over outrigger	sailors: etc.	100
draft:	6ft.	marines	2900

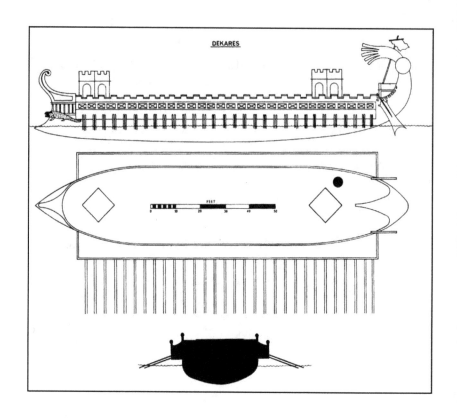

DEKARES

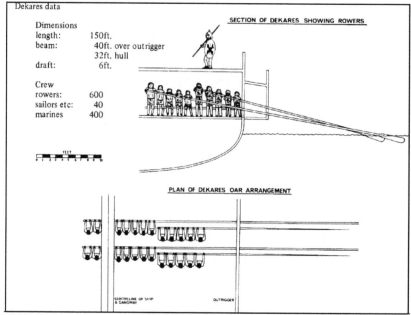

Dekares data

Dimensions
length: 150ft.
beam: 40ft. over outrigger
              32ft. hull
draft: 6ft.

Crew
rowers: 600
sailors etc: 40
marines   400

SECTION OF DEKARES SHOWING ROWERS

PLAN OF DEKARES OAR ARRANGEMENT

ROMAN DEKARES lst CENT. B.C. `ANTONIA'

This ship is typical of the largest vessels in the fleets of the Roman Civil Wars in the lst century B.C. There are two levels of oars, almost on the same level, with the ten rowers disposed 5 plus 5. Because of the length of the oars, not all the rowers can sit throughout the stroke, and some must stand to pull, as illustrated in the sectional drawing.

The vessel is designed for boarding tactics, and in addition to the towers shown, will certainly have carried dart throwers. The towers cover the probable boarding points at bow and stern, and appear to be set at 45° to the axis of the ship, so that the face of the tower is towards the probable direction of attack. Such towers were collapsible, and would be jettisoned by a defeated fleet to aid escape. In the fleets of Octavian and Sextus Pompeius, the colours of the towers were standard throughout the fleet, and served as a means of identification of friendly vessels.

The figurehead is a crocodile. Sculpture or carving on a vessels bow often denotes the ships name, as with modern figureheads, but the crocodile was the symbol of Egypt, so it might equally indicate an Egyptian vessel. Cleopatra's flagship at Actium was the Antonia.

The vexillum was the mark of a Roman flagship, and remained up day and night, and whether the admiral was aboard or not. When two admirals met at sea, however, the junior would lower his flag, part of a complicated naval ceremonial scantily recorded for posterity.

We do know, however, that when a Roman magistrate took to the sea, his chief lictor preceded him just as on land, but in this case by standing in the bows of the ship with his fasces!

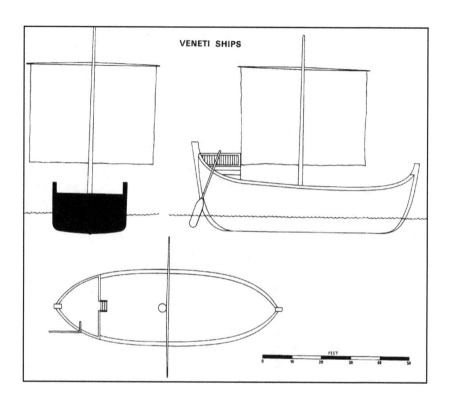

VENETI SHIPS

FEET

0   10   20   30   40   50

VENETI SHIP 1st CENTURY B.C.

The Veneti, the Celtic tribe inhabiting the NW coasts of Gaul, dominated the Atlantic and Channel until their subjugation by the Romans. Their strength is shown by their being able to produce a fleet of over 200 warships.

Their ships differed considerably from the Roman vessels opposing them, and the points of difference are described by Caesar.

They were propelled by sail, not oars, and were of very stout oak construction (Roman and other Mediterranean ships used fir or pine mainly) with chain anchor cables. Both bow and stern, stern especially, were very high, and the latter was higher than the tower on a Roman warship. The sides of the ships were also high enough to give the crew an advantage over Romans. This suggests that the stern rail must have been at least 20ft. above the water.

A vessel discovered at Blackfriars, dating from a couple of centuries later, is very similar to the description given by Caesar, and suggests that this type of vessel continued in use in northern waters, as a merchant ship.

The vessel illustrated is based on Caesar's description, and the dimensions of the Blackfriars ship. A single mast and square sail is given.

The lack of harbour facilities made the flat bottom necessary, as ships would normally be grounded at low tide in a sheltered spot for loading or unloading. Commius the Atrebate, fleeing to Britain from the Romans, found himself still aground with the pursuers in view, in such a ship as this. He cunningly ordered sail to be set, although still high and dry, and the Romans, thinking he was under way and out of reach, called off the pursuit.

A cabin is shown at the stern, on which the helmsman stands, controlling one long steering oar. The cabin roof also gives elevation to the fighting men, when the vessel is used for war.

Veneti ship data

Dimensions	Crew
length: 75 ft.	5/10 sailors
beam: 24 ft.	50/60 fighting men
draft: 5 ft.	

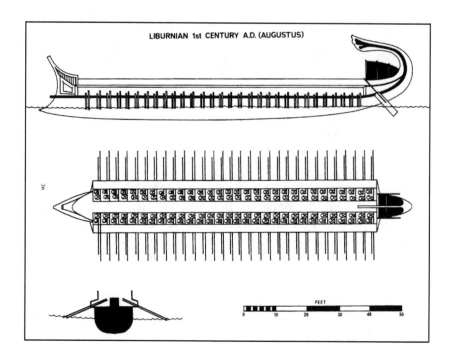

LIBURNIAN 1st CENTURY A.D. (AUGUSTUS)

FEET
0   10   20   30   40   50

LIBURNIAN   1st CENTURY A.D.   `RADIANS'

This is a typical smaller galley of the period, based on paintings and mosaic representations. A bireme, here reconstructed with 60 oars per side and 120 rowers, and no complete deck over the oarsmen, this is probably the vessel referred to as a liburnian.

Liburnians were originally light vessels used by Illyrian pirates, which were copied by the Romans, but the name seems to have changed meaning over the years, and may have come to denote any ship which was not cataphract.

This type of ship supported the heavier ships in battle and acted as a scout. It was probably the type of vessel used by Caesar in his campaign against the Veneti, and for the invasion of Britain.

The ship has a leather shelter in the stern, and some are shown with a sternwalk. `Radians' (Brilliant) is recorded as the name of a ship of the Classis Britannica.

Liburnian data

Dimensions
length: 120ft.
beam: 15ft. over outriggers
12ft. hull
draft   3ft.

Crew
rowers: 120
crew etc.   10 approx.
marines 40 approx.

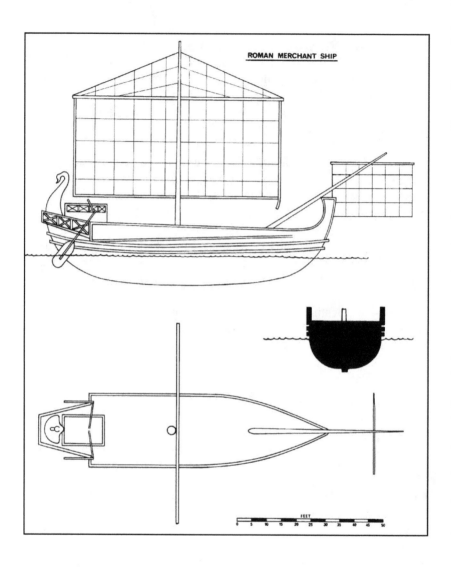

ROMAN MERCHANT SHIP

FEET
0 5 10 15 20 25 30 35 40 45 50

ROMAN MERCHANTMAN 1st CENTURY A.D.   'EUROPA'

This is a typical Roman merchant vessel of the lst Century A.D. In size it is not larger than the earlier Greek ships, but there are several differences in detail.

Most noticeable are the two masts, the foremast carrying a small foresail, chiefly for use in steering. There is also a triangular topsail above the mainsail, and this sometimes appears above the artemon as well.

The stern of the vessel is also different. There is an upcurved sternpost in the form of a goose head (the sacred bird of Isis, patroness of sailors) and a sternwalk round it. The bulwarks at the side of the ship at the stern quarter stand out from the hull, and from them the steering oars are pivoted. There is a cabin at the stern, and the helmsman stands on the roof of this cabin, controlling both oars by means of long handles. Long substantial wales run down the sides of the ship, and must have given substantial strength to the hull.

The largest ancient merchant ships of the period were used to carry grain from Alexandria to Rome; a typical ship of this type, the Isis, was 180ft. long and had a capacity estimated at over 1200 tons. The vessel illustrated is of the more usual size, to judge by wrecks found, and has a capacity of about 100-150 tons. Such ships went all over the Mediterranean carrying general cargo.

Roman Merchantman data

Dimensions
length: 100ft.
beam: 25ft.
draft: l0ft.

Crew
sailors: 10/15

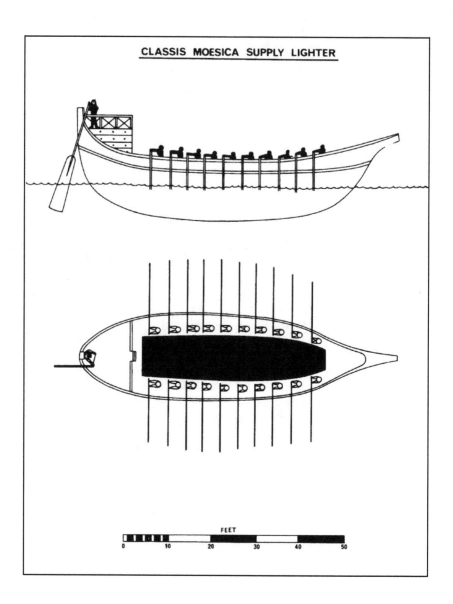

CLASSIS MOESICA SUPPLY LIGHTER

CLASSIS FLAVIA MOESICA SUPPLY LIGHTER   100 A.D.

Trajan's column illustrates some of the supply and logistic arrangements of the Roman Army, in this case provided by the Moesian Fleet, based on the lower Danube.

The type of lighter or barge illustrated is ubiquitous. It has an open hold, and is propelled by sweeps. No mast or sails are shown. There is a wooden cabin at the stern with a railing round the top. The helmsman stands on the roof of this cabin and controls a single long steering oar.

Such a craft, although slow, might easily carry 50 tons of cargo, and would be the best method of carrying the quantity of supplies needed for a major campaign. The Column shows ships carrying both bales (grain sacks?) and barrels (ration wine or olive oil). Wine was normally conveyed in amphorae commercially - perhaps the army used different methods with the large quantities they needed.

These lighters are also shown carrying horses, and forming the supports of pontoon bridges. To make a bridge, a number of craft were moored alongside each other across the river and the bridge roadway ran on piers of wood built up from the hold.

The absence of sails makes it a fair inference apart from the uniform pattern that these craft were specially constructed for the Fleet. Craft for civil use would not be built requiring expensive rowers to propel them.

Apart from transporting men, horses and supplies, Roman fleets played an important part in campaigns by supplying skilled craftsmen for engineering work, particularly in timber. Fabri Navales probably made ordinary bridges as well as the pontoons already referred to.

Supply Lighter data

length: 72ft.
beam.   20ft.
draft: 7.5 ft.
carrying capacity 50 tons
Crew   25 maximum

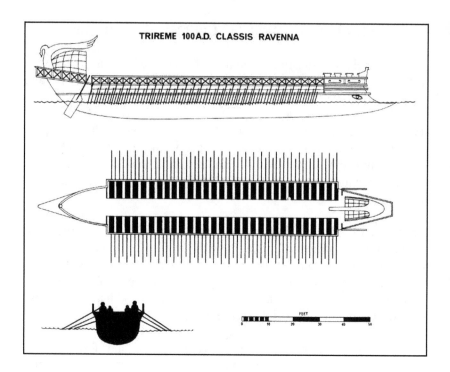

Trireme data

Dimensions		Crew	
length:	140 ft.	rowers:	180
beam:	20 ft. over outrigger	sailors etc:	20
	16 ft. hull max.	marines:	70
draft:	3 ft.	Total	270

TRIREME   RAVENNA FLEET 'CONCORDIA' 100 A.D.

This vessel is based on examples shown on Trajan's column. The size of ship and general arrangement of the rowers is similar to that in the Classical Greek Trireme, but there are a number of differences of detail. The vessel is more substantial in appearance and the side of the ship where the oars appear is not open, but solid. There are no parablemata; instead a railing with X shaped struts runs along the top of the parekseiresia, and a similar rail round the stern is part of a stern gallery. A large leather shelter protects the helmsman and officers on the stern.

The manning of these vessels and others of the Imperial Fleets was a curious mixture of traditional Greek naval practice and Roman military methods. The old officer ranks remained, translated to Latin as:

kubernetes – gubernator

keleustes - pausarius

proreus - proreta

However, each ship was organised as a Century on the army pattern, and all the army ranks, including the signifer and the various trumpeters, were found among the crew.

The captain of the ship was a Trierarch, irrespective of whether the ship was a trireme or some other rating, and he corresponded to a centurion in the army. It is not clear whether the trierarch had to contend with an army centurion on the ship, at least equal to him in rank, or whether he was himself referred to as centurion; there is a reference to the senior officers of ships as the `centurions and gubernators', which suggests this. In this case, the Trierarch/Centurion was the captain, with the Gubernator his senior assistant on the seaman side, and the Optio senior assistant with the marine contingent. Imperial Roman ships were organised in Fleets, each of which patrolled a particular territory. The Ravenna Fleet's area was the Adriatic. The commander of a Fleet was a Prefect, who usually had no previous naval experience, but was appointed by the Imperial government. Under him were Navarchs, each controlling a squadron probably of 10 ships.

Fleets contained ships of all sizes up to 6 Banks - these latter were Fleet Flagships. As no major hostile navy was in being, the trend was towards open ships, not cataphract, as illustrated. Triremes were the standard warship and for river flotillas were the flagships. Peacable abstracts like Concordia were favourite ship names with the Imperial Fleet.

BIREME CLASSIS BRITANNICA

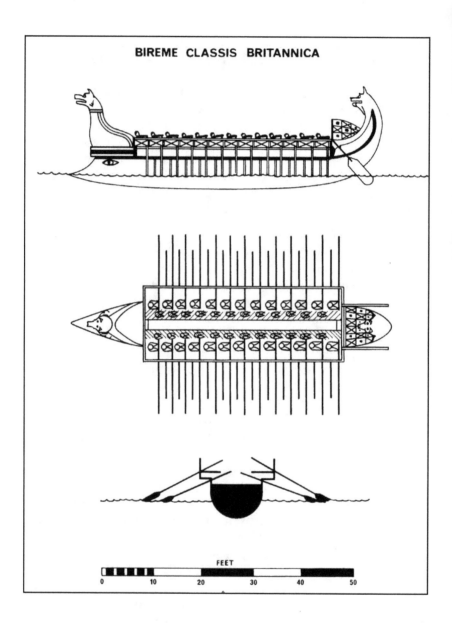

FEET

0   10   20   30   40   50

BIREME - CLASSIS BRITANNICA 250 A.D. 'SABRINA'

Roman ships in northern waters found conditions very different from the Mediterranean, and ships of normal Mediterranean type suffered severely from weather and tides. Julius Caesar lost a large part of the invasion fleet on the south coast of Britain, and Germanicus later lost many ships in a storm at the mouth of the Rhine.

Although the fleets established on the Rhine and in the Channel and North Sea continued to use galleys (including some triremes), these were modified to take into account the sea conditions encountered, and higher sides and bows were the rule. The illustration shows a bireme of the Classic Britannica of the 3rd Century AD. This ship is typical of the later Roman period, and appears to represent a development of the Classical type of galley, modified for use in northern waters.

The bireme has 50 rowers, 26 in the upper bank with their oars projecting through the railings on top of the outrigger, and 24 in the lower bank with oars coming through the ships side under the outrigger. The upper oarsmen are visible from the ship's side; the lower oarsmen sit inboard of them, staggered, and about 2'6" lower.

The ship has a freeboard of 4ft. to the outrigger and lower oars (3 ft. was perhaps more normal in the Mediterranean), and with leather askomata round the lower oars the effective freeboard would be 6ft.

There are the usual double steering oars and leather shelter for the steersman. The stern does not have the usual railed walk round it, but this may have been present on other ships. Both bow and stern end in carved wolf heads, a fairly common feature of ships in the north western Imperial fleets at this period. Some vessels had the ram also in the form of an animal's head.

Such ships were also used for the transport of supplies. Wine in barrels is one of the cargoes shown being carried. The second section drawing of this ship shows how barrels could be carried down the centre of the vessel by removing the lower bank of rowers.

'Sabrina' is the Roman name for the Severn: "river" names were common for Roman Imperial warships.

Bireme data

Dimensions		Crew	
length:	65ft.	rowers:	50
beam:	15ft. over outrigger	sailors etc:	10 approx.
	10ft. hull max.	marines:	20
draft:	3 ft.	Total	80

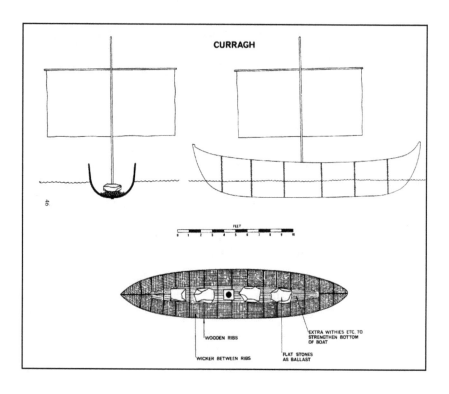

CURRAGH

WOODEN RIBS

WICKER BETWEEN RIBS

EXTRA WITHIES ETC. TO
STRENGTHEN BOTTOM
OF BOAT

FLAT STONES
AS BALLAST

THE CURRAGH

The Curragh is a ubiquitous Celtic boat, used for both river and sea voyages. Boats of this type were used in Britain and Ireland from perhaps the 4th century B.C. until at least Mediaeval times, and the somewhat similar coracle is still in use today.

The curragh is constructed of a keel and ribs of wood, with the hull between the ribs filled in with wickerwork. Over the whole, and to make it waterproof, a skin envelope is placed, made of several hides sewn together.

The curragh illustrated is one of the largest types, being 20ft. long, and equipped with a mast and square sail. Paddles provided the alternative means of propulsion. To ballast the boat large flat stones are placed in the bottom on top of withies. It is suggested that these stones gave rise to the alleged miracles of Irish saints sailing across the sea on millstones.

Curraghs regularly sailed from Britain to Ireland and on the journey no supplies were carried. In the Dark Ages even longer journeys were undertaken.

The curragh was also used on at least one occasion by the Roman army. In 49 B.C. Julius Caesar had his soldiers construct curraghs in Spain to cross a river; his campaigns in Britain having made him familiar with the type of vessel.

In later times a curragh would be a suitable means of transport for small raiding parties of Picts or Celts. More formidable forces would tend to use wooden vessels of larger size.

Curragh data

Dimensions
length: 20ft.
beam: 4ft.
draft: 1-1.5 ft.

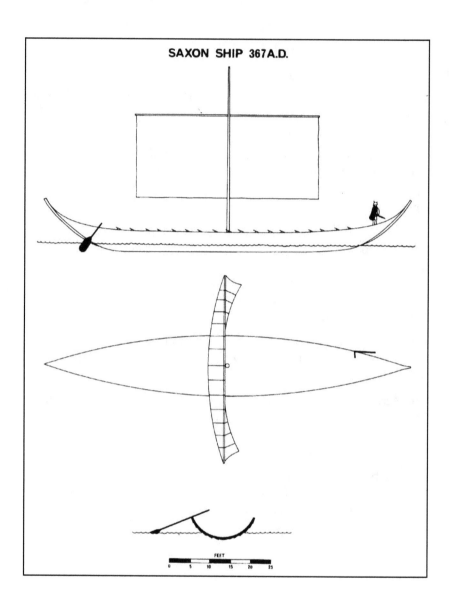

SAXON SHIP 367A.D.

FEET

0   5   10   15   20   25

SAXON SHIP 367 A.D.

This is a typical ship of the Saxon peoples who raided in the North sea in the late Roman period and later.

This ship is a large open boat, clinker built, with provision for 36 oars. A large square sail is carried. It has been thought that Saxon vessels did not carry sails, but sails were well known in the Southern North Sea and Channel among both Romans and Barbarians, and it is not conceivable that major raids could have been carried out along the British coast by vessels relying on oars alone.

However it certainly appears to be the case that the sail was not generally used in what is now Norway, Sweden & Denmark until the Viking period.

The Saxon vessel had no keel; the keel being merely a flat plank, similar to the planks forming the hull. Certainly originally the hull planking was tied to the ribs; later vessels were nailed.

The double ended shape is typical of all northern ships, and continues with Viking and other vessels.

Steering is by means of a single steering oar fixed to the starboard (steer-board) side of the vessel. This is universal with northern ships, in contrast to the double oars of the Mediterranean tradition.

A ship such as this is mainly a means of transporting fighting men, and in a sea battle would be no match for a Roman galley, the latter with its multiple banks of oars developing far more speed and power, as well as having more height in a boarding battle.

Saxon vessels from rowing boats upwards all have the same general hull shape and design as the vessel shown here, varying only in size and number of oars.

Saxon ship data

Dimensions
Length 90 ft.
Beam 15 ft.
Draft   2ft.

Crew
Rowers 36
Others   15

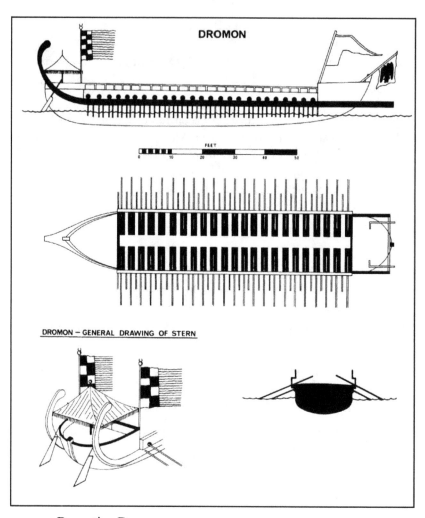

DROMON

DROMON – GENERAL DRAWING OF STERN

Byzantine Dromon

Dimensions	Crew (pamphylos)
Length 120 ft.	Rowers 150 (100 with body armour)
Beam 20 ft.	Marines 35
Draft 4 ft.	Sailors etc. 20
	Total 205

The breakup of the Roman Empire created a break in the continuity of ship design. For a period smallish vessels only were built, and the typical merchant ship and warship designs both disappeared. Small merchant vessels, perhaps 50-60 ft. long with simple bow and stern, almost double ended in shape, and with lateen type rig, were perhaps the norm. When therefore the Eastern Roman Empire again constructed major fleets, the appearance of the warships was very different from that of earlier times.

BYZANTINE DROMON   800 A.D.

The standard warship was called the Dromon. Almost invariably it had 25 sets of oars per side, invariably it was 2 banked. The lower oars were always manned by one rower only; the upper by one, two or three men, the ships being called ousiakos, pamphylos, and dromon respectively, depending on the number of upper bank rowers. The vessel illustrated is a pamphylos. The hull shape is much more slab sided than on earlier warships, and the outrigger is therefore rudimentary. There is no deck protecting the upper rowers, but the high sides give them some defence against missiles, and they wore armour in addition. The wales along the side of the ship are carried up to form a double tail, and continue forward to form part of the ram. The ram itself has moved above the waterline into the position it occupied throughout the later history of galleys, and is now a crippling rather than ship killing weapon. The dromons were equipped with lateen sails; Belisarius' flagships in the expedition to Africa had the upper part of the lateen sail coloured red as identification. There were probably 2 masts on most dromons, each with a single sail, but the biggest may have had three. These masts and sails stayed up in battle instead of being struck as with earlier ship

From the middle of the 7th Century A.D. the main offensive weapon of the dromon was a flamethrower or throwers projecting Greek Fire. The flamethrower took the form of a bronze siphon often in the form of an animal's head. The primary location was in the bows firing forward; subsidiary devices were located in the ships beam.

Byzantine dromons carried a force of marines with body, thigh and arm armour, armed with lance, javelin and sword, and a large part of the rowers were similarly armed. They were supported by light archers and slingers, and once in contact with an enemy the whole crew seems to have taken part in the boarding fight, in contrast to earlier battles, when rowers and marines were separate. The largest dromons carried towers amidships as well as at bow and stern; those amidships projected beyond the level of the ships side.

The dromon was the standard battleship of the Byzantines; it was also used by the Goths and later by the Arabs, neither of whom were especially skilled at naval warfare. The Arabs indeed used the Viking tactic of chaining the whole fleet together on occasion, nullifying the superior Byzantine seamanship. For scouting duties the Byzantines used a vessel with oars on one level, called a galea or galley. This vessel gradually became bigger until it reached the size where it became the standard warship, and the dromon became obsolete; it was still being used extensively at the time of the Crusades, however, by both Christians and Saracens.

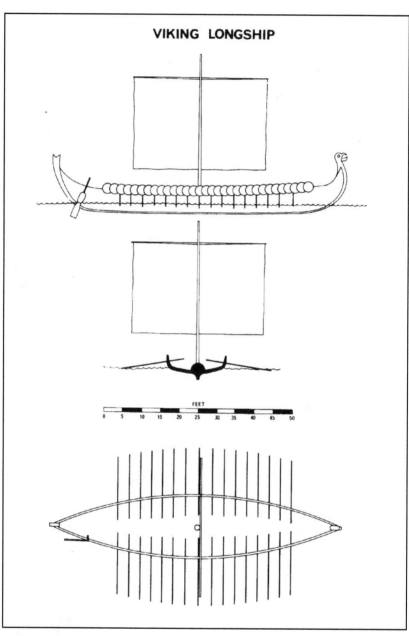

VIKING LONGSHIP

Viking longship data

Dimensions	Crew
Length 78ft.	Rowers 64
Beam 17ft.	Others 10-11
Draft 2.5ft.	Total 75, all of whom
Height of mast 42ft.	are fighting men

VIKING SHIP 850 A.D.

The vessels of the Scandinavian peoples in the early part of the Dark Ages appear to have been without sails, but by 750 AD vessels equipped with sails were beginning to enable the Viking peoples to voyage forth in search of plunder.

A number of ships of the Viking period have now been found in various states of preservation, and the appearance of the ships is well known.

Viking ships took the form of open, clinker built boats, keeping the usual northern double ended form. They were equipped with a mast, which could be raised and lowered, and a single square sail, often brightly coloured with particoloured vertical bands.

The chief difference from the earlier Saxon boats are that the shape of the hull is more refined, and in particular that there is now a proper keel, which must have considerably aided the sailing qualities. Replicas of Viking vessels have proved themselves extremely seaworthy.

The ship illustrated is a longship or warship, with 16 oars per side. Each oar is manned by 2 men, so that there are 32 shields belonging to the crew on each gunwale to protect the rowers. The steersman controls a steering oar on the starboard side of the vessel. At the bow the stem (more curved than with the Saxon ships) terminates in a dragon's head. The oars appear through ports in the hull instead of over the gunwale, giving higher freeboard.

Longships varied considerably in size. The largest recorded are a vessel of Olaf Tryggevasson called the Long Serpent, which had a keel length of 122 ft. and an overall length of about 150, and a ship of King Canute which had 60 rowing benches, which, unless this means 30 per side, would require a length of nearly 200 ft. The Long Serpent had 8 men per half room and 30 extras; this makes her the equivalent of a Greek or Roman `8', and her crew total a minimum of 574. But the Long Serpent was an exception, and the vessel here illustrated is the typical Viking longship, as far as size is concerned.

The longship was not the only type of Viking vessel. Merchant ships (Knarrs) also existed, and it was in these types of ship, not warships, that the voyages of exploration and colonisation were undertaken. The knarr was more solidly constructed than a warship, with higher sides and greater beam in relation to length (maybe 3.5:1) but preserved the same general method of construction and appearance.

Part II: Ancient Naval Campaigns.

This part of the book deals with ancient naval campaigns with the aim of illustrating the range of different situations found in ancient naval warfare and the development of tactical and other ideas.

Not every naval battle has been included, and some well known fights have been neglected in favour of lesser known actions which better illustrate the progress of naval tactics.

As with ship types, ancient evidence is sometimes very scanty as far as battles are concerned, and different interpretations have been put on many well known battles by different authorities.

The reconstructions of battles given here are based upon the ancient authorities, and represent the best assessment of the evidence which can be made.

To supplement the accounts of individual battles, a chronological chart has been given, detailing the main historical events coupled with the progress of the naval art.

NAVAL TACTICS

Ancient naval tactics had two distinct sets of exponents, one school favouring manouevre and the use of the ram, the second regarding ships purely as personnel carriers, from the decks of which soldiers would board the enemy.

Although the Ram school had many successes, it was eventually boarding tactics which were supreme. This was because the only ship killing weapon available was the ram, which required contact to be made with the enemy; which was of course exactly what the boarding school desired.

The ram was a feature of galleys long before tactics were devised for it's use as a major weapon. Formal tactics may have been invented by the Phocaeans about 500 BC; they were certainly fully developed in the Athenian navy by 430 BC, by which time Athenians considered boarding tactics very old fashioned.

The essence of ramming tactics was to outflank the enemy and ram him in the beam. Two formal tactics were devised to bring this about, the Diekplus and the Periplus. Both assumed that the enemy would adopt the usual formation of line abreast, and both were based on manouevre in line astern.

The Periplus consisted of a move round the enemy's exposed flank so as to fall on his rear. The Diekplus involved passing between the ships of the enemy line, breaking off oars while passing through, then turning to attack the enemy's vulnerable rear, as with the Periplus.

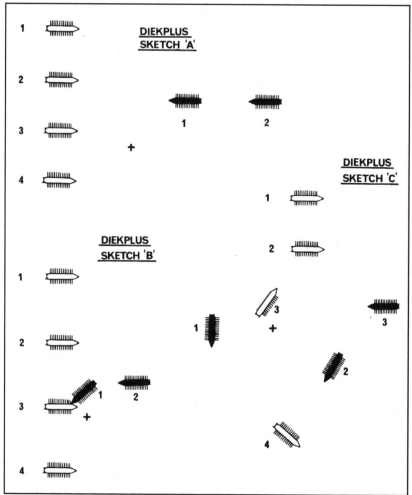

The Diekplus in particular was a tactic for small groups of ships or even individual vessels as well as whole fleets to adopt.

These manouevre tactics were obviously the prerogative of skilled and highly trained fleets, whose ships had an advantage in performance over their opponents. The tactics also gave much greater control to an admiral. The rudimentary signalling methods available, and their limited range, meant that a fleet in line abreast could only conform to some previous plan, or carry out a limited range of previously foreseen alternatives. A fleet in line astern with the Flag leading had only to conform to the admiral's movements.

It is worth while to consider the Diekplus in detail, as it represents the summit of manouevre tactics, and from it the various countermeasures devised by admirals of the board school derive.

Sketch A shows two opposing squadrons, white in line abreast, black in line astern and about to carry out a diekplus. Black is moving fairly fast; white is also under way, but at a slower speed.

Sketch B shows the moment of contact. Black one aims for the gap between white 2 and 3, and puts the helm hard over, bringing the bow into contact with the port side of white 3.

Sketch C shows the situation a few seconds later. Black one has continued on round to port and is about to pick up way again. White 3 has lost the port oars and the effect of this and the impact with black one has swung the ship round to port. The ship is crippled and may have sprung a leak as well. Black 2 could ram and sink White 3, but instead has turned and is trying to ram White 4, which has turned away to starboard. Black 3 is moving up in support. White 1 and 2 are in a difficult position. They could turn to starboard to attack Black 2 & 3, but if they do this they will expose their beams to Black 3's supports coming up. In fact Black has succeeded in creating a melee in which the faster and handier Black ships have every advantage.

The essential factor is the superior performance of the Black ships, and in particular Black one (the Flagship), in making the initial break between the White ships, a manouevre calling for the most skilful judgement.

This then was the Diekplus. Naval tactics after the diekplus developed only as ways of countering it and the similar tactics used by skilled fleets.

The first counter to the Diekplus was quickly devised; the defending fleet simply put a second line of ships behind the first. This made it suicidal for a ship to carry out the Diekplus, as it would find itself broadside on to the ships of the enemy second line, and would inevitably be rammed.

Unfortunately the provision of a double line was likely fatally to shorten the distance from wing to wing, and thus make it easy for a skilled fleet to carry out a periplus.

An ingenious development of this idea was used by the Corinthian admiral Machaon, facing the Athenian Phormio in the Gulf of Patras in 429 BC. Machaon formed up his ships in a large circle, prows outward, with a reserve of five ships in the centre of the circle to thwart any attempt at diekplus. This provided both second line and secure flanks, and would have been unbreakable by manouevre if it had been possible to maintain the formation. However the Athenians sailed in line astern round and round the circle, continually presenting a series of possible ram targets to the Corinthians, which could not be attacked without splitting the formation. The Athenian movement also served to compress the enemy circle, and when a breeze got up (as expected by Phormio) the enemy were unable to maintain their formation and began to drift into each other, giving the Athenians the opportunity to attack.

Although this particular formation had failed, the Corinthians persisted in trying to find a counter to the Athenian tactics. A Corinthian, Polyanthes, found a method of dealing with Athenian ships in narrow waters which led directly to the Athenian disaster in Syracuse harbour.

Polyanthes idea was to strengthen the epotides of his vessels, and deliberately seek to ram bow to bow. Epotis is normally translated 'cathead'; in fact the epotides were the forward cross timbers forming the front of the outrigger. On an Athenian vessel these were as light as possible. The Corinthians strengthened the bows of their vessels and their epotides, and provided a ship which could cripple an Athenian in a bow to bow ram without itself suffering damage. In such a ram each ship's stem would tend to come to rest on the enemy's epotis, and if the epotis were damaged, this would mean that the outrigger on that side of the vessel could no longer support oars.

A seriously outclassed fleet might (particularly if supported by an army) merely run its ship's sterns up a beach, prows out to sea, and fight a boarding battle against the enemy. The difficulty with this formation was that all mobility was lost and the enemy could concentrate all his force against one part of the defending line.

A further refinement therefore was to adopt a convex formation, with the end ships flanks on the shore, all afloat, and some room for movement behind the centre.

No counter was however devised to manouevre tactics in the open sea, although such tactics became more difficult to apply, the larger the number of ships in action. A fleet of 100 ships in double line abreast at 50 yd. intervals between ships would present an unbroken front 2,500 yds. long, and only the flank ships would be vulnerable to manouevre tactics. Intervals between ships varied: probably 20yds was the interval where both sides were planning to board.

The Hellenistic navies preferred boarding tactics, and the increasing size of warships was largely governed by a desire to have as many marines as possible; the larger polyremes had no advantage in speed or manouevrability over smaller vessels, and the trireme and quadrireme probably were the fastest and most manouevrable ships in antiquity.

The development of dart and stone throwing engines did little to alter naval tactics. Engines were found to be effective against ships when used as shore batteries, but when mounted on ships were only an adjunct to the boarding battle, as a stonethrower large enough to cause serious damage to a ship was too heavy to be practical, when carried by a battleship.

A major development which permitted a boarding fleet to overcome a fleet relying on manouevre was made by the Romans, when they set out to challenge the Carthaginian command of the sea at the beginning of the 1st Punic War. The disadvantage of manouevre tactics was that ramming involved close contact with the enemy; the Roman invention of a machine called the corvus or raven was designed to arrest any vessel coming in to ram, hold it, and permit the Roman marines to board.

The Corvus itself had disadvantages and was soon dropped, but it was the forerunner of a series of similar Roman devices, all with the same purpose, and all given the generic name of Ferrea Manus or Iron Hand.

Opposite is an illustration of the corvus, reconstructed according to the description of it given by Polybius. A pole 24ft. long and 12" in diameter has a pulley at the top. The pole stands on the prow of the ship, and the pulley enables a gangway to be lifted and dropped.

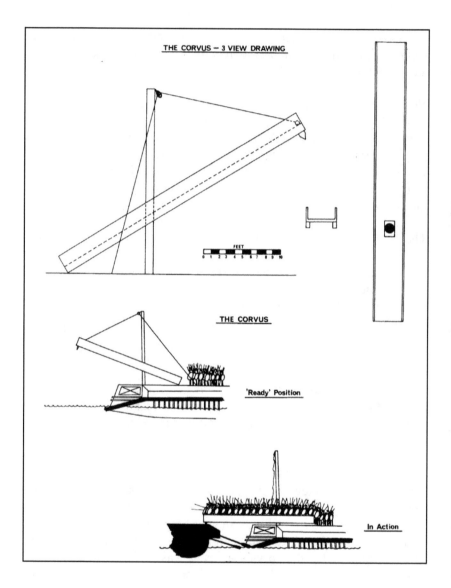

THE CORVUS – 3 VIEW DRAWING

FEET

THE CORVUS

'Ready' Position

In Action

The gangway is 36ft. long, and has an oblong hole 12ft. from one end through which the pole rises. At the outer end of the gangway is an iron ring to hold the line from the pulley, and under the gangway a heavy iron spike to hold the enemy ship. On engaging an enemy, the marines (80 legionaries) would move 2 abreast down the 4ft. wide gangway and board the enemy.

Ancient authors do not give the disadvantages of the corvus, but it soon fell into disuse. Once the initial surprise had been lost, its unwieldy character and limited traverse must have made it easy to evade, and as Roman seamanship improved, it represented too much of a performance handicap.

In the early years of the 2nd century BC, the Macedonian fleet made a further contribution to solving the problem of beating a manouevre fleet. Large numbers of lembi - small open boats with about 30 crew - supported the main battle fleet. Lembi were as good a deterrent to the diekplus as a second line of battleships, and could harry an enemy and smash his oars. Furthermore, they were very cheap, and easy to man. The 300 rowers required by a 5 could equally man 10 lembi.

Lembi had the disadvantage of being vulnerable to major ships on their own, and their superiority over such vessels was only in manouevrability.

At about the same period the Rhodian fleet invented the firepot. This was a bronze container holding fire held on a long beam from the bow of a ship. If an enemy approached, the fire would be dropped onto his deck.

The use of firepots was partly an aid to manouevre tactics, and the Rhodians found that an enemy faced with firepots would sheer off rather than come in for a bow to bow ram, and firepot on the foredeck; which of course exposed the vulnerable side of the ship to the Rhodian rams.

It was Octavian's admiral Agrippa who devised the next method of getting a boarding fleet in contact with an elusive enemy. This was the logical culmination of the Roman series of grapnels, or Iron Hands, and was called the Harpax. Simple in conception, it was merely a grapnel designed to be fired by a dart thrower; an enemy, caught at a distance, could be hauled alongside and boarded. But if the enemy had scythe blades on long handles, the Harpax lines could be cut.

The establishment of the Roman Empire, and the disappearance of any first class enemy from the Mediterranean, stopped the development of naval tactics at this point, with the board school• in the ascendant. When warfare again commenced between civilised powers, in the Byzantine era, the contrast in tactics emphasises the break in continuity. The shipkilling ram has been moved above the waterline for use as a crippling weapon, and the emphasis is on archery and heavily armed marines.

The Byzantine navy shortly established a tactical superiority over their Arab opponents with a new weapon, Greek Fire. Of secret (and probably variable) composition, this was an incendiary mixture, difficult to extinguish, projected through a bronze siphon in the form of an animal's head. With an effective range of perhaps 50ft, it was nevertheless the first long range ship killing weapon.

Meanwhile in Northern waters, the Vikings had brought boarding tactics to the ultimate; preferring to lash their ships together into a huge floating island, over which the combined crews, iron clad and axe in hand, could roam, daring anyone to board. But the Vikings seem always to have considered ships purely as means of transport and fighting platforms, not as weapons in their own right, and the same probably holds true for the Saxons earlier.

The use of sailing ships poses a problem: we simply have not sufficient evidence of tactics used by powers like the Veneti. Probably boarding after exchange of missiles was all that was done. Boarding after the rigging had been cut with scythes on poles was the effective counter adopted by Caesar's fleet.

THE PERSIAN WARS

The westward advance of the Persian Empire in the 6th Century BC brought under its control the Greek cities of the coast of Asia Minor. Here, Persian rule was highly resented; not so much because the Persians were oppressive; indeed their rule was mild and the stability they brought to the Middle East considerably aided commercial states. It was rather the Persian support for local dictatorships, or tyrannies in the Greek word, and their harbouring tyrants expelled from independent Greek cities, which made them appear a menace to the Greeks.

The origins of the Persian wars lie therefore in the revolt of the Greek cities of the Ionian coast.

In 499 BC they rose in revolt and expelled their tyrants. They formed a league which directed the war, and sought allies from the cities of independent Greece.

In 498 BC the Ionian League, with assistance from Athens and from Eretria in Euboea (20 and 5 ships respectively), sent an expeditionary force which burnt Sardis, seat of the Persian satrap, whilst their ships spread the revolt as far as Cyprus.

The Ionian fleet aided the Greek cities of Cyprus when a large Persian army and fleet invaded the island to recapture it. The principal city of the island was Salamis, and the opposing fleets and armies met near that city.

The Ionian fleet defeated the Phoenician squadron which was supporting the Persian army, but the Persian army, aided by the treachery in the Greek forces which was a common feature of these wars, defeated the Cypriot army, and the Ionians could do no more than return home.

By 494 BC the Persians were pressing back into Ionia by both land and sea, and threatening Miletus, the hub of the revolt. The last chance of survival for the league was their fleet, which was concentrated at the island of Lade, near Miletus, and was threatened by a Persian fleet of 600 ships.

The bulk of the fleet was provided by Miletus, and by the inhabitants of the three big islands off the Ionian coast, Samos, Lesbos, and Chios. There were a number of smaller contingents, however, ranging down to the 3 ships provided by Myus and the 3 by the city of Phocaea.

It was the commander of the Phocaean contingent, Dionysius, who attempted to bring some efficiency to the allied fleet, and for a few days he was able to have them at exercises and began to train them in manouevres like the diekplus, which were obviously previously unfamiliar to them. Soon however the fatal Greek independence of character came into play, and the other contingents refused to follow Dionysius, spending their time idling on the island of Lade.

There was also treachery in the Greek ranks. When the Persian fleet came, the Ionians set out to engage. Although not nearly well enough trained for it, their vessels were in the formation for the diekplus of line astern; this probably means columns of about 10 ships.

Nothing is known of the Persian formation, but their superiority in numbers will have allowed them a considerable overlap, particularly on the seaward wing (the Greek right). Although they were able to dispose of 600 ships, they may have had considerable difficulty in getting all of them into action or formed up, particularly if they were not using a column formation.

The plan shows what happened in the battle. The Samians on the Ionian right, who were probably greatly outflanked, did not engage, but broke for home before the battle started, except for 11 ships, which stayed and fought. The Lesbians next to the Samians fled when their flank was uncovered in turn, and part of the Greek left wing also fled at this stage.

The centre, namely the Chians, stayed and fought hard, both taking and inflicting heavy casualties. They were equipped for a boarding battle, having 40 marines per trireme, and Greek hoplites were better marines than Persians.

The Persian left wing must have set off in pursuit of the Lesbians and Samians, because there was no attempt to surround the Ionian centre. The survivors of the Chian contingent were able to retire to their own

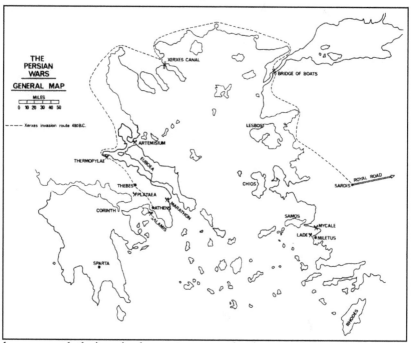

homes, and their cripples got across the bay to the north shore at Mycale.

Most successful of the Greeks was Dionysius of Phocaea. His 3 ships must have been the best trained in the fleet, and a gap in the Persian line opened opposite him when their left set off in pursuit of the Greek right. He was therefore able to break through, and took three enemy ships, apparently without loss to himself. It was however clear that the day and cause were lost.

(Dionysius' subsequent exploits were interesting. Instead of returning home he set out for the Phoenician coast, denuded of warships with the Persian fleet in Ionia, and engaged in some very profitable commerce raiding with his fleet of 6 ships, before moving to Sicily, and setting up as a buccaneer there.)

The battle of Lade was the end of the Revolt, apart from mopping up. The Persians next turned to revenge against those cities which had aided the Ionians in the burning of Sardis, Athens and Eretria; behind the plan was the extension of Persian rule over Greece.

In 492 BC the Persian Mardonius conquered Thrace and Macedon and secured the land route to Greece. In 490 BC a fleet of 600 triremes plus horse transports brought a Persian army across the Aegean.

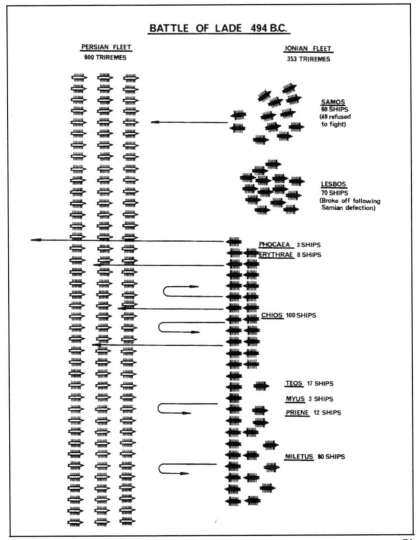

BATTLE OF LADE 494 B.C.

PERSIAN FLEET
600 TRIREMES

IONIAN FLEET
353 TRIREMES

SAMOS
60 SHIPS
(49 refused
to fight)

LESBOS
70 SHIPS
(Broke off following
Samian defection)

PHOCAEA 3 SHIPS
ERYTHRAE 8 SHIPS

CHIOS 100 SHIPS

TEOS 17 SHIPS

MYUS 3 SHIPS

PRIENE 12 SHIPS

MILETUS 80 SHIPS

After subduing various islands they took Eretria and then landed in Attica at Marathon.

The Athenian army here defeated the Persians (which at 40 fighting men per trireme could have totalled 25,000 men), and then foiled an attempt by the Persian Fleet to convey the survivors round Attica to seize Athens, by a rapid march back to the city from the Marathon position.

There then ensued a lull of 10 years; the Persians were distracted by a revolt in Egypt, among other factors. Towards the end of that period, however, it became obvious that the Persians were going to make a major effort to conquer the Greek mainland, and a number of states in northern and central Greece were prepared to submit to them. For once the Greeks combined their forces, under the leadership of the Spartans, the foremost military power, and prepared to resist.

The Persian army massed by King Xerxes probably consisted of about 100,000 fighting troops, including the 10,000 Immortals, the King's Guard. The fleet had over 1,000 warships, the entire muster of the eastern Mediteranean, plus a horde of supply ships. The great force set off from Sardis, and crossed the Dardanelles by pontoon bridges provided by the fleet. To avoid the ships having to round the dangerous Athos peninsula (where a Persian fleet had been wrecked 10 years before) a canal was dug across the base of the peninsula.

The Greeks originally intended to defend northern Greece, but in the event the land forces were placed in the pass at Thermopylae, and the fleet held the entrance to the channel between Euboea and the mainland at Artemisium.

The strategy of the campaign was simple. Both sides were aware that at close quarters the hoplites and the Greek ships were superior to the Persians. The Persians nevertheless had the numbers to overwhelm their opponents. The Greek aim was therefore to hold a narrow position where their flanks were secure; the Persians to find a way round to enable their numbers to be brought to bear.

At Thermopylae after three days a traitor showed the Persians the way round. The fleet at Artemisium they equally sought to outflank; immediately on arrival a force of 200 ships was sent to sail round Euboea to attack the Greeks from the rear.

The Greek force at Artemisium consisted of 271 triremes, plus a few obsolete pentekonters. This fleet was made up of 127 Athenian ships (in the years following Marathon the Athenians had diverted the increasing revenue of the Laurium silver mines to the building of a fleet), 40 Corinthian, 20 from Megara, 20 from Chalcis (supplied by Athens, but manned by Chalcis) and 64 from nine other states. The Persians had over 1,000, less the flanking force, but the Greeks were forced to send 53 Athenian ships to the narrowest part of the Euripus between Euboea and the mainland to hold off the flank force. Although the Spartans only provided ten ships, their admiral, Eurybiadas, had the command of the whole fleet; although Athens provided the largest contingent none of the others would serve under an Athenian admiral.

The Greeks had a stroke of good fortune before the Persians moved into the strait; a storm arose which not only drove many of Persian ships ashore, but also destroyed the flank force sailing round Euboea. The odds were thus evened by the loss of well over 200 Persian vessels and by the return to the main fleet of the 53 Athenians who had been guarding the Euripus.

The Persian were not only more numerous but had better trained crews, and thus the advantage in manouevre. On the first day the Greeks therefore tried a novel formation, which presented no open flank, and did not permit a diekplus. They formed up in a large circle, prows outwards. The Persians lost 30 ships in the first days fighting, and gained no advantage. The second day was quiet, with the Persians at Aphetae apparently awaiting a result either from the land engagement or from their flanking force. During the course of the day the 53 Athenians came up from the Euripus, and it must have been clear to the Persians that their outflanking force was lost.

On the third day the fleets met again, and neither side had a decisive advantage, but the Greek fleet continued to hold up the Persians. At least 100 Greek ships had now suffered some damage, and more than that number of the Persians. At the end of the day, however, news came to the fleet that the Spartans at Thermopylae had been overrun, and there was no further bar to the Persian army advancing into Greece. The Fleet accordingly withdrew.

The Greek land forces now held and were building a wall across the isthmus of Corinth, which meant the abandonment of Thebes (which submitted to the enemy) and Athens. Most of the population of Athens was ferried to Salamis, Aegina and Troezen, and the Fleet based itself at Salamis following the retreat from Artemisium.

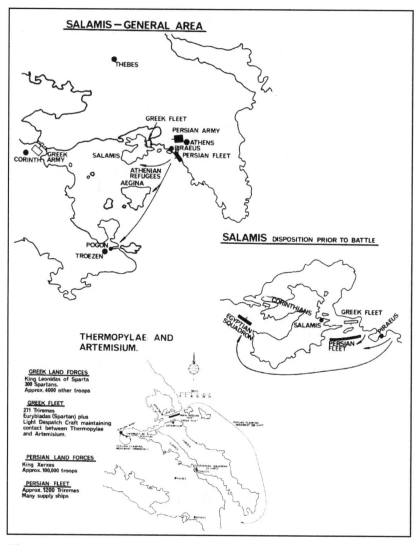

The Persian fleet had also advanced and was based on the open beach at Phaleron, before Athens, and on the adjacent beaches and harbours.

The Persians were reluctant to enter the narrow waters between Salamis and the mainland, after their experiences at Artemisium, particularly as the Greek fleet had now been brought up to 380 ships, with reserves which had been mustering at Pogon, the port of Troezen. The Athenians, however, were having difficulty in inducing their allies to remain at Salamis; the Peloponnesians were pressing hard for a retreat to the Isthmus to join the army, which would have meant abandoning the Athenian refugees.

The Persians were nevertheless determined to prevent the Greek fleet escaping from the Salamis position. The situation was precipitated, according to the account of Herodotus, by the Athenian commander, Themistocles, who passed a message secretly to the Persians informing them that the Greeks were planning a withdrawal. This induced the Persians to get their fleet to sea to block the exits to the east and west of Salamis. Themistocles then informed the Greek admirals that a fight was inevitable.

The Persian initial dispositions were: facing the western exit, the Egyptian squadron, originally 200 strong, now perhaps down to about 150. Facing the eastern exit were the remainder of the fleet, of which the core was now the Phoenician and Ionian squadrons. The Phoenicians had originally provided 300 ships, and the Ionians 100. In addition the Persians put a garrison onto the island of Psyttalea, to gain possession of any damaged vessels that were beached there in the course of the battle. To oppose the Egyptian squadron, and hold the western exit, the Greeks placed the Corinthians, probably with other vessels, maybe 80 ships in all. The remainder of the Greek fleet was at the eastern exit, where the main decision was to be sought.

The Persian fleet was disposed to meet an expected Greek breakout. The Greek plan was to entice the enemy into the more confined waters of the strait, where their inferiority in numbers would be less critical.

The fleet therefore left its anchorage on the north side of the Cynosura peninsula, and set off eastwards, before turning south and forming line facing the Persians. The latter advanced to engage, and the Greeks backed water into the narrows of the strait.

The effect of this manoeuvre was to entice the Persians forward, so that they had to split their formation to pass round Psyttalea island, and then were forced onto a narrow frontage. When the Persians passed north of the line of Cynosura they were also presenting a flank to the Greeks.

The engagement itself lasted for a number of hours, but at the end of the day the Greek fleet was victorious, despite the hard fight put up by the Persians, conscious of the presence of Xerxes himself watching the battle from a height overlooking the strait.

Meanwhile the Corinthians had been in action at the other exit against the Egyptians, and had prevented that force from carrying out the outflanking movement (similar to that at Artemisium) with which it had been entrusted.

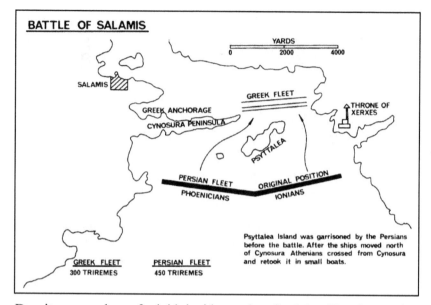

BATTLE OF SALAMIS

YARDS
0   2000   4000

SALAMIS

GREEK FLEET

GREEK ANCHORAGE
CYNOSURA PENINSULA

THRONE OF
XERXES

PSYTTALEA

PERSIAN FLEET
PHOENICIANS

ORIGINAL POSITION
IONIANS

Psyttalea Island was garrisoned by the Persians before the battle. After the ships moved north of Cynosura Athenians crossed from Cynosura and retook it in small boats.

GREEK FLEET
300 TRIREMES

PERSIAN FLEET
450 TRIREMES

Despite a number of vivid incidents described by Herodotus, the actual course of the battle is so difficult to reconstruct that various authors have the Greek fleet facing north, facing south, and facing east. The battle only makes sense, however, if the Persians took position in waters favourable to them to prevent an expected Greek breakout, and were then enticed past Psyttalea in the narrow waters of the strait. The strait itself is about 2,000 yds. wide, and we are told the Greeks were in 3 lines. This would leave about 20ft. between the tips of the oarblades of adjacent ships, which is very close, assuming 300 Greek ships in total. However, the larger Persian fleet would be even more congested, and could not use its numbers effectively. The result of the battle was that the Persian fleet retired to Asia Minor, and Xerxes retreated, leaving a land army in northern Greece.

In the year 479 BC this land army was defeated by the Greeks at the battle of Platea, and in the same year the Greek fleet crossed the Aegean, and destroyed the remains of the Persian fleet at its winter base at Mycale.

This resulted in the reconquest by the Greeks of the Ionian islands and mainland cities over the next few years, and it was not until 448 BC that peace was formally signed between the Greeks and Persia.

Following the victory at Salamis the Greek admirals met to vote who had done the most for the cause of freedom in the War. When the votes were counted it was found that every admiral had voted for himself ....

BATTLE OF PATRAS 429

This battle represents the manouevre tactics of the Athenian navy at their summit, when small expert squadrons were handled together under a single admiral.

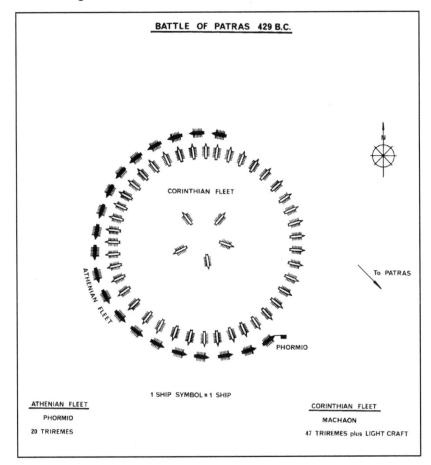

BATTLE OF PATRAS 429 B.C.

CORINTHIAN FLEET

ATHENIAN FLEET

To PATRAS

PHORMIO

1 SHIP SYMBOL = 1 SHIP

ATHENIAN FLEET
PHORMIO
20 TRIREMES

CORINTHIAN FLEET
MACHAON
47 TRIREMES plus LIGHT CRAFT

In the early years of the Peloponnesian War, the Athenians established a naval base at Naupactus in the narrows of the Gulf of Corinth, and allied themselves with various states on the north side of the Gulf, with the object of hindering the trade of Corinth with Sicily and the west. In 429 BC the Athenians had a squadron of 20 triremes at Naupactus under Phormio.

The Peloponnesians sent an abortive expeditionary force against the Athenians under a Spartan commander, and in addition dispatched a Corinthian squadron of 47 ships to invade the north shore.

The Corinthian squadron under Machaon moved along the south side of the Gulf, shadowed by the Athenian squadron, until it reached Patras. From Patras it set out at dawn to cross the straits, and halfway across was intercepted by the Athenian force.

Although far superior in numbers, Machaon knew that his ships were no match for the Athenians in open water, particularly since his ships were burdened with a great deal of equipment for the invasion.

He accordingly adopted the formation which had been used successfully by the Greeks at Artemisium against superior Persian ships, and formed his ships in a large circle, rams outwards. 42 ships formed the circle; the small craft and the five best triremes were in the centre as reserves. It was early in the day and the sea was calm.

Phormio's fleet was in line astern formation, and he led it round the Corinthian circle like a band of Indians attacking a waggon train. The Athenian ships continually feinted attack on the Corinthian ships and tempted them to charge. This would of course have been fatal to any Corinthian who tried it, as he could not get under way quickly enough to hit his target, and any ship leaving the circle would itself immediately present a ram target to the Athenians.

The effect of Phormio's tactics was therefore that the enemy tightened their formation even more.

As the morning wore on, the wind got up, which had been expected and counted on by Phormio. The effect of the wind and the waves which got up was devastating on the Corinthian formation. Being stationary in the water, they could not maintain formation, and began to drift into each other, and the swell made things difficult for their inexperienced oarsmen. In a short time the impeccable formation was in chaos, and the Athenians attacked.

Machaon could do nothing but turn to flee, with his formation broken up, and the Athenians took 12 ships in a pursuit back to the south shore of the Gulf.

It is often said that fleet manouevre tactics of the type used by Phormio fell into decay after this period. If this is so it is not because any dramatic counter to them was found, but rather that fleets were larger. Phormio had only 20 ships, which in a single column must still have been about 1000 yds long, which approaches the useful limit; any longer and individual ships at the back would take too long to get up to where the action was. It is therefore general increase in the number of ships deployed, not any decrease in seamanship, which caused the manouevre tactics on a fleet basis as used here to fall into disuse.

THE WAR FOR THE AEGEAN 412-405 B.C.

In 413 BC the great Athenian expedition to Syracuse was destroyed, and the flower of the Athenian navy was lost. Up to this period the Peloponnesians had been unable to challenge Athens effectively at sea, the only element in which she could be decisively defeated. From 413 to 405 BC a naval war was fought in the Aegean, with the object of gaining control of Athens allies, the source of much of her wealth, and more important, seizing the trade route by which the grain ships from the Black Sea fed the population of Athens, secure in the impregnable fortress of Athens and Piraeus.

The combatants were however by no means ranged on two sides, and there were in fact four different parties, with divisions within these parties.

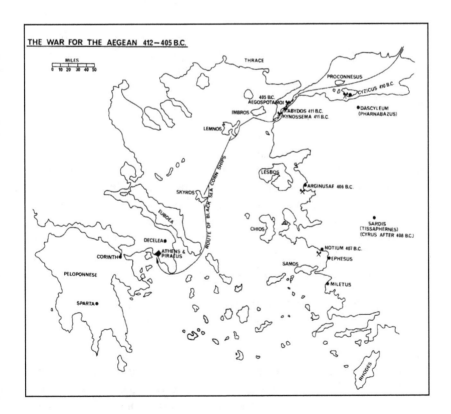

First are the Athenians, masters of the Aegean islands and the coast of Ionia, and the foremost naval power of Greece. The Athenian side however included:

(a) an oligarchic party which for part of the period gained control of the city of Athens and was sympathetic by background to the oligarchs of the Peloponnese.

(b) The fleet, predominantly manned from the poorer classes and democratic in tendency. When the oligarchs were in control of Athens there was an independent democracy in exile at the main fleet base at Samos, claiming to be the true Government of Athens.

(c) the Allies, originally members of a free League against the Persians which had been converted into an Athenian Empire, and eager for a genuine opportunity to recover their freedom.

The leaders of the Peloponnesians were the Spartans, who were the traditional military leaders of Greece, and commanded the fleets of the Peloponnesians, although providing a minority of the ships. The Spartans were much less anti Athenian than their allies, and following the final defeat of Athens, succeeded in imposing relatively moderate terms. This was in contrast to Corinth which sought to have Athens utterly destroyed. Spartan prosecution of the war was often half hearted, and they made several armistice proposals.

These two were the main protagonists. Supporting the Peloponnesians were the Persians. The Persians were seeking to recover the territory lost in the Persian Wars, and to weaken the power of the Greeks. Persia provided no naval force, but had apparently unlimited subsidies to pay one side or the other, and was perpetually promising the intervention of a fleet from the eastern Mediterranean, which never came. Persia was represented by two local Satraps, at Dascyleum and Sardis, and by the central government of the King of Kings, and each of these parties pursued an independent line.

Pharnabazus was the satrap of Daseyleum, and a strong pro Spartan until forced by Athenian successes to cease his support.

Tissaphernes was Satrap of Sardis. The most devious of the Persians, he saw that the aims of Persia might best be served by keeping both Greek sides fighting for as long as possible, with the end result of a Greece exhausted by a long war. He therefore supported both sides alternately. Unfortunately Tissaphernes had powerful enemies in the Royal family, who had him transferred in 408 , and later executed.

Cyrus, son of the King of Kings, was sent in 408 as overlord of the Ionian coast to Sardis. A young man, he was influenced by the dynamic Spartan commander Lysander, and gave the Peloponnesians exclusive support.

Finally there was Alcibiades. Alcibiades was one of the most gifted and prominent Athenians of his day, and a prime mover of the Sicilian Expedition. Exiled at the start of this expedition, he had defected to Sparta, and was serving their interests in trying to foment a revolt among Athens allies in 412 . He subsequently returned to the Athenian side as Commander in Chief, but throughout appears to have been pursuing a policy of personal aggrandisement alone, aimed at securing his supremacy in Athens.

The first map shows the area of the war. In general, Athens controlled the islands, which were either allied or, in the case of Euboea, Skyros, Lemnos and Imbros, which were strung out along the Black Sea supply route, held by Athenian colonists. The Peloponnesians were effectively restricted to the coastline of Asia Minor, and their main bases were at Ephesus and Miletus.

The year 412 and the first half of 411 passed without major conflict; the Peloponnesians were establishing their forces, somewhat hampered by Tissaphernes, who was giving them only half hearted aid. At the end of 411, however, the Spartan commander, Mindarus, realising that Tissaphernes was not genuine, resolved to break north, and base himself upon the more certain aid from Pharnabazus.

This forced the Athenian fleet at Samos to follow, since a Spartan fleet in the Hellespont would effectively block the trade route. At Kynossema in the Hellespont 76 Athenian ships met and defeated 86 Peloponnesian, including a Syracusan squadron, and later in the year there was a further battle near Abydos, where 74 Athenian vessels engaged 97 Peloponnesian. In this engagement the battle was in doubt until a further 18 vessels commanded by Alcibiades (by now back in the Athenian fold) came up, and the Peloponnesians beached their vessels, and defended them on the shore line with the aid of a Persian land force under Pharnabazus, but lost 30 towed away as prizes.

These two battles effectively restored Athenian morale and confidence in their naval supremacy, and in the following year the strategic situation was turned in their favour. The Spartans and Persians began the year by taking the city of Cyzicus (then on an island). The Athenian fleet had dispersed for the winter, but collected together, and passed up the Hellespont by night. After leaving their sailing gear on the island of Proconnesus, and seizing all small craft to prevent news of their arrival being carried to Cyzicus, the Athenians set out to seek the enemy.

The weather was bad, unusually for an ancient naval battle, with heavy rain and very restricted visibility. The result was that Mindarus, the Spartan commander, who had set out with his 60 ships to engage in manouevres, found as the weather cleared that the Athenians with 86 ships were between him and his base at Cyzicus.

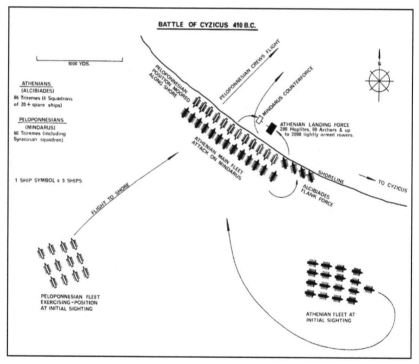

Recognising his inferiority in both numbers and skill, Mindarus immediately set off for the shore, and moored his ships, as at Abydos the previous year. It appears that Persian soldiers from Cyzicus also started out to assist him.

The Athenians, however, had superiority of numbers, unlike the situation at Abydos. They were thus able to oppose the enemy on a one for one basis, while Alcibiades with 20 ships carried out a Periplus, and landed in their rear. Mindarus attempted to land to counter this move, but was killed, and a general panic ensued, with the

Peloponnesians abandoning their ships and fleeing inland. Assuming that Alcibiades landed all his marines and the rowers from two out of the three banks of oars, he could have put ashore 200 hoplites, 80 archers, and up to 2000 rowers with light arms.

The battle of Cyzicus was the end of the Peloponnesian attempt to take the Hellespont area; following the battle Mindarus' successor sent a message of classic Laconic brevity back to Sparta – "Ships lost. Mindarus dead. Men starving. Don't know what to do." The reply is not recorded, but Sparta made an armistice offer to Athens which was rejected.

For the next three years the scene of action changed to the southern front. In 408 Tissaphernes was replaced by Cyrus at Sardis, and under a vigorous Spartan commander, Lysander, the Peloponnesians built up a fleet backed by Persian money. Alcibiades in the meantime had been made Commander in Chief of the Athenian forces, but following the defeat of one of his subordinates by Lysander at Notium in 407 BC, he was again sent into exile.

In 406 BC Lysander handed over his office to his successor, Callicratidas. Callicratidas was a bluff Spartan, brave and honest, and quite unsuited to the diplomatic task of negotiating with the Persians. He was quite up to Lysander, however, and when the latter handed over

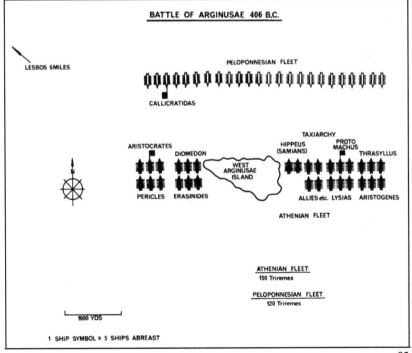

command, claiming Command of the Sea, Callicratidas merely suggested he should take the fleet from Ephesus to Miletus (past the main Athenian base on Samos) and repeat his boast.

Callicratidas however very soon fell out with the Persians and resolved to prove that he could win a campaign without their assistance. With Lysander's carefully built up fleet, plus further reinforcements, totalling 170 ships, he set off to try to capture the town of Methymna on Lesbos, being shadowed perforce by Conon, the new Athenian commander on Samos. Conon had only 70 ships, but first class vessels and crews. He was however blockaded in Mytilene on Lesbos by Callicratidas' superior numbers, and Callicratidas took Methymna.

The Athenian strategic situation was desperate. The only fleet was blockaded in Mytilene, and Callicratidas had effective control of the Aegean. With a vast effort, the Athenians manned every ship left in any kind of seaworthy condition in the Piraeus; even slaves were empressed, showing the seriousness of the situation. 110 ships left Athens for Samos, where a further 40 reinforcements were added, and the relief force set off up the coast of Asia Minor.

When Callicratidas heard that a relief force was on the way, he left 50 ships to maintain the blockade of Conon, and set off with 120 to engage the new arrivals.

The Athenians had 150 ships as opposed to the 120 of the Peloponnesians, but took up a defensive position, in view of their inferiority in seamanship. Their position was based upon the Arginusae islands, about 7 miles S.E. of Cape Malea on Lesbos, where Callicratidas was based. The Arginusae islands lie of the coast of Asia Minor.

Because of the inferior seamanship of the reserve fleet, the Athenian formation was a double line, to counter a diekplus by the enemy. This would have resulted in their line being shorter than that of Callicratidas but for the presence of the western Arginusae island, which formed the centre of their line. At one length intervals between ships, the 80 Athenian vessels in the front line would have covered about 3,200 yds. This, plus the 1,600 yds. of the island equals the front occupied by the 120 Peloponnesian ships, which were in single line abreast. Evidently by this time fleet or squadron diekplus tactics were out, but the manouevre was practised by single ships.

Since the Athenian dispositions prevented any Peloponnesian manouevre tactics, the battle was a hard fought melee. Callicratidas himself had according to Xenophon the misfortune to fall overboard with the shock of his ship ramming another, and was drowned, and his fleet lost 69 ships or nearly 60%. Athenian losses were 25.

The Athenians had once again completely restored their position, therefore, although the Spartan commander facing Conon skilfully extricated his now seriously outnumbered command and escaped.

In the next year however, Lysander returned in effective command of the Peloponnesian fleet. He patched up the diplomatic breach which Callicratidas had made with the Persians, and manned with Persian gold a fleet of up to 200 vessels. With a grasp of the strategic essentials, he took his fleet straight to the Hellespont, the Athenian lifeline, took the city of Lampsacus, made it his base, and awaited developments. Since Cyrus in Sardis was now effective overlord of all Persian resources, this transfer from the area of one Satrapy to another was not as difficult as it would have been previously.

The Athenian fleet, 180 strong, had to react to Lysander's challenge, and moved to the opposite side of the Hellespont, taking position on open beaches about Aegospotami, the Goats Rivers. This was a bad position, as the crews had to go some distance to get supplies, but the Athenians were expecting Lysander to meet them almost immediately at sea. Both sides drew up their forces daily, but did not engage, neither seeing an advantage.

On the fifth day, Lysander waited until the Athenian crews had beached their ships and set off in search of supplies (which they had to buy themselves) and then launched his whole fleet again, and fell upon the Athenian ships in their exposed position.

Only 9 ships under Conon, the best of the Athenian admirals, were fully manned, and escaped; the rest were captured, together with 3,000 of their crews. Almost by default, the Athenian naval power was broken. Unable to man another fleet, and with the supply route cut, Athens was starved into surrender within a year.

Lysander had Pharnabazus arrange the assassination of Alcibiades, who had taken refuge in his territory.

THE BATTLE OF SALAMIS 306 BC

This battle marks the first victory by the big Polyremes which became a feature of most of the Hellenistic fleets, and it is fitting that the winning fleet should have been commanded by Demetrius Poliorketes, who was the main developer of these vessels.

The circumstances leading up to the battle may be briefly described. Antigonus, the father of Demetrius, was attempting to reunite the Empire of Alexander under his own leadership, and was at war with Ptolemy of Egypt. Demetrius had invaded the island of Cyprus, which was held for Ptolemy with 60 ships and 12,000 men by his brother Menelaus. He defeated Menelaus and besieged him in the city of Salamis, the principal one on the island.

Ptolemy left Egypt with a relief force of 140 warships, 200 transports, and 10,000 soldiers, which he took directly across the open sea to Paphos in Cyprus (the route up the Syrian coast was in enemy hands, but this movement direct shows that Greek fleets were not necessarily coastbound, although it was more convenient to land at frequent intervals).

Ptolemy's relief force now moved eastwards towards Salamis, while he and Demetrius exchanged messages, each offering the other terms which were unacceptable. The situation of Demetrius was critical; he had only 108 warships, superior numbers to Menelaus, but very much

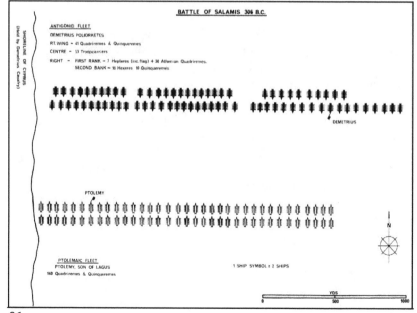

less than Ptolemy, particularly if Ptolemy made a junction with his brother.

The battle of Salamis which followed was fought south of the city as Demetrius aimed at a crushing victory to prevent the Egyptian forces joining. Ptolemy was very near to Menelaus when Demetrius moved.

Demetrius left only 10 Fives to face Menelaus' 60 ships - which were probably Fours and Fives - but the exit to Salamis harbour was narrow, so they had a good chance of holding him. With the rest of his fleet he moved to face Ptolemy. To make up for his opponents superiority in numbers, Demetrius put his own troop carrying ships into the battle line, 53 in number. These were not merchant ships, but may have been a hybrid type; there were vessels called phaseli which had merchant ship lines and 3 banks of oars. More probably, they were old warships with some of the rowing benches removed and perhaps extra decking. This would permit them to carry troops for the boarding battle which Demetrius intended, and their lack of speed would not be a handicap under the circumstances.

The actual dispositions of the two fleets are shown on the plan. Demetrius was concentrating his main effort on his left (seaward) wing, where his best and heaviest ships were. These included seven Hepteres and ten Hexeres, bigger and heavier than any ship Ptolemy had. Putting the 53 transports into the line enabled Demetrius to extend his left beyond Ptolemy and outflank him.

As a further innovation, Demetrius' ships were carrying artillery, both dart and stone throwers, to fire into the enemy marines clustered on deck at a distance.

Finally, the shore line was firmly held by Demetrius' cavalry, ensuring that the crews of any crippled ships which ran ashore would fall into his hands, a ship by itself being much less valuable as a prize than with its crew of 3-400 men.

The battle itself went largely according to Demetrius' plan. His left swung round and bottled up the Ptolemaic fleet against a hostile shore, and 120 of the enemy were taken. Ptolemy himself broke through Demetrius right with a few ships, but found when he had done so that the battle was already lost, and fled. Only 20 of his ships got away, and 8,000 of the troops he had brought with him were captured.

Menelaus took some time to break past the 10 Demetrian ships at the harbour mouth, and by the time he got to the scene of battle, he could do nothing. He retired to Salamis to negotiate terms of surrender.

The victory of Demetrius gave him the island of Cyprus and command of the sea for 20 years.

THE FIRST PUNIC WAR

The First Punic War saw control of the Western Mediterranean pass from the Carthaginians to the rising Roman Republic, and indeed represents the major naval effort by the Roman Republic.

The war was a long one, lasting 20 years, with (surprisingly, since the main theatre of war was an island) both sides at various stages letting their fleets decay.

The object of the War was the control of the island of Sicily, previously shared by Greeks and Carthaginians, occupying the eastern and western ends respectively. The actual reason for the outbreak of war (a dispute over certain unsavoury mercenaries called Mamertines) is unimportant; the main matter is that the Romans determined to extend their influence over Sicily, and set out to construct a fleet to do it. This meant a direct challenge to the Carthaginian navy, numbering about 200 quinqueremes, and manned by a people with a long and honourable seafaring tradition.The Romans had had a minor fleet of a score or so of triremes; now they built a battlefleet of 100 quinqueremes and 20 triremes. They are said to have used a captured Carthaginian vessel as a model, and in the days when shipbuilding was a matter of individual shipwrights experience, not plans on paper, they must have had some vessel for the carpenters to copy, but it cannot have been a typical Punic ship, because Roman vessels were consistently slower and heavier than Carthaginian until a fast prize was taken and copied later in the war.

At any rate, the Romans prepared their fleet, and in 260 BC set off to Sicily to engage the Carthaginians. They did have one major tactical surprise in the corvus (fully described in the tactics section), and an excellent force of marines. Legionaries were particularly suitable for duties as marines, their flexible individual fighting tactics being ideal for shipboard.

Despite the loss of several ships in a preliminary skirmish, the Romans met 130 Punic ships at Mylae. The Roman commander was the Consul, C. Duilius; the Carthaginians were commanded by one of the innumerable Hannibals in Punic history.

The Carthaginians boldly attacked, and lost 50 ships to the Roman boarders before withdrawing. Their losses included Hannibal's flagship, a 7 captured from Pyrrhus of Epirus, and the admiral himself narrowly escaped in the ship's boat. He might have been better off in Roman hands, for in the next year he was again defeated by the Romans in Sardinian waters, and his subordinates showed their displeasure in the usual way by crucifying him.

Following Mylae there was little naval activity for two years. Then in 257 BC there occurred a small skirmish which both sides believed they had got the better of.

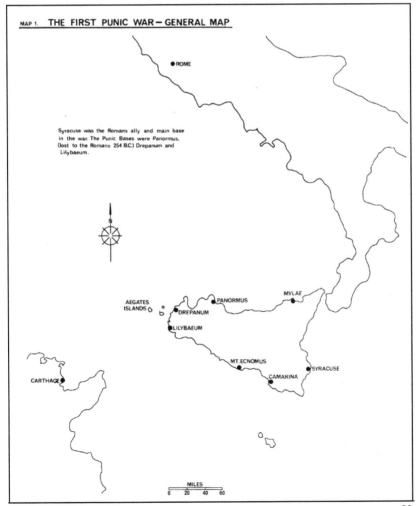

MAP 1. **THE FIRST PUNIC WAR – GENERAL MAP**

Syracuse was the Romans ally and main base in the war. The Punic Bases were Panormus, (lost to the Romans 254 B.C.) Drepanum and Lilybaeum.

Both therefore determined on a big effort for the year 256 BC

The Roman plan was for an invasion of the Carthaginian home land, bypassing the unconquered part of Sicily. A fleet of 330 cataphract ships was prepared, and a rendezvous with the army arranged near Mt. Ecnomus in southern Sicily.

The Carthaginians had no less than 350 ships, according to Polybius, which if correct was an outstanding effort, as their normal muster was 200. This fleet moved to the south coast of Sicily to a position enabling them to intercept the Roman invasion fleet.

The ensuing Battle of Ecnomus illustrates clearly the typical tactics of both fleets, and is of interest for the elaborate set plans drawn up by the opposing admirals.

The plan of the battle illustrates the initial dispositions.

The Roman fleet was commanded by the two Consuls, M. Atilius Regulus and L. Manlius, each of whom had a 6; the rest of the fleet will have been 5's. The usual consular army was 2 legions, and this system was transposed to the sea, with each Consul commanding 2 squadrons. The fleet was thus split into four equal units.

The Romans were hampered by their transports, carrying the horses, and to nullify the known Carthaginian advantage in seamanship they devised a kind of box formation, containing and covering the transports.

Leading the Roman formation were the two Consuls, Manlius on the right, Regulus on the left, side by side, with a squadron (legion) in single line echeloned away on either side. Across the base of the triangle thus formed was the 3rd Squadron, which was towing the transports, and behind the transports was the 4th Squadron, somewhat spread out so the ships of this unit overlapped and protected the flanks of the 3rd Squadron. This 4th Squadron the Romans, using military terminology wherever possible, called the Triarii.

The Carthaginian fleet was commanded by an admiral called Hamilcar, who devised a plan strikingly similar to that employed so successfully 40 years later at Cannae. The fleet formation was a single line abreast, which must have covered about 3 miles of sea. Hamilcar, with about half the fleet, held the centre. A subordinate called Hanno

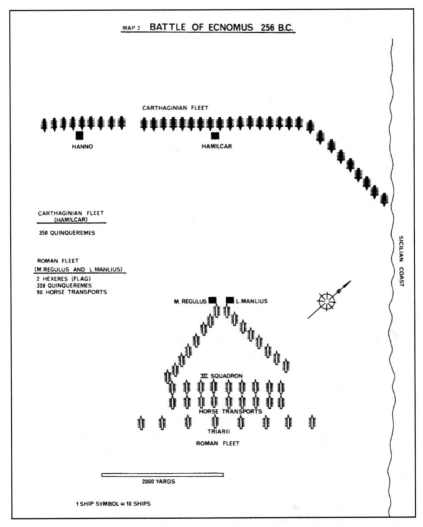

MAP 2 BATTLE OF ECNOMUS 256 B.C.

CARTHAGINIAN FLEET

HANNO

HAMILCAR

CARTHAGINIAN FLEET
(HAMILCAR)

350 QUINQUEREMES

ROMAN FLEET
(M.REGULUS AND L.MANLIUS)
2 HEXERES (FLAG)
328 QUINQUEREMES
90 HORSE TRANSPORTS

M. REGULUS   L.MANLIUS

III. SQUADRON

HORSE TRANSPORTS

TRIARII

ROMAN FLEET

SICILIAN COAST

2000 YARDS

1 SHIP SYMBOL = 10 SHIPS

commanded a Fast Squadron on the right (seaward) wing; the left wing was angled somewhat forward of the rest of the fleet.

The battle began with the Punic center backing water, acting on orders. The Consuls pressed forward to try to make contact, and in doing so a gap inevitably opened between their two units and Squadron 3 towing the horse transports.

When Hamilcar felt that a sufficient gap had been opened, he signalled the attack, and his squadron turned to engage the Consuls, while the two Punic flank squadrons moved forward onto the Roman flanks.

The 3rd Roman squadron was corvus equipped, and no match for Punic ships in the open sea. Abandoning the transports, it took up a position on the shore line with sterns to the land, threatening to board anyone coming in close. The Triarii squadron swung left and began to engage Hanno's Fast Squadron. The transports were left unprotected, and must have started trying to get out of the way.

The Romans would have suffered a naval Cannae, if the Punic centre had held. But the Romans defeated Hamilcar, whose ships were less suited than the Romans' to a holding action of this type, and while Manlius secured prizes and saw the enemy centre off, Regulus returned to the aid of the Triarii, who were being badly handled by Hanno's crack squadron. Hanno could not contend with two Roman squadrons, and was forced to retire in turn. Then Manlius returned to the battle and the Romans penned the Carthaginian left, still facing the Roman 3rd squadron.

This was the end of the battle, in which the Consuls lost 24 ships sunk (probably mostly from the Triarii, and representing over a quarter of that squadron), while the Punic losses were 30 sunk, probably mainly from Hamilcar's centre, and 64 ships captured. At least 50 of the prizes came from the encircled left wing, which started the battle about 80 strong.

The Carthaginians did not attempt to dispute the Roman victory, and the Invasion Force landed in Africa, apparently neutralising the Punic fleet for a time, as the manpower had to be diverted to the land forces, in defence of the homeland.

The skill of a Spartan mercenary General, Xanthippus, and the overconfidence and ambition of the Consul in Africa, Regulus, resulted in the defeat of the Roman forces, whose remains were restricted to their base at Aspis. The Carthaginians then manned a fleet of 200 ships for the next year.

The Consuls for 255 BC (Aemilius & Fulvius) took a relief fleet of 350 ships, which crushed the numerically weaker Punic fleet, taking 114 prizes, and rescued the survivors of the invasion force.

Returning in triumph, with the command of the sea decisively confirmed, the Consuls, sailing in autumn along the rocky south coast of Sicily against the advice of their experienced seamen, encountered a storm. The fleet was driven onto the rocks and 284 ships out of the total number of 364 were lost. Even if half the crews were saved, this represents a loss of 60,000 men.

The Romans nevertheless started rebuilding, and the Carthaginians were again tempted to dispute the command of the sea, and were further encouraged by another naval disaster in 253BC, when the Consuls Servilius and Sempronius, after a sereis of futile raids on the African coast, and having to jettison all their heavy equipmentafter running the entire fleet aground, decided to cross the open sea from Panormus to the Tiber. They encountered a storm and lost 150 ships!

No major naval activity nevertheless ocurred until 249 BC when the Romans were besieging the major Punic base of Lilybaeum. While their fleet was present at the siege, it was not preventing faster Cathaginian ships from regular bockade running from the Agatian Islands or from keeping a substantial fleet at Drepanum, about 15 miles north of Lilybaeum; indeed many of the rowers were being used as labourers in the siege works and had been lost in the fighting on land.

The situation was altered by the arrival of 10,000 reinforcements to the fleet, under P. Claudius Pulcher, who remanned the ships and took command. His plan was to raid the Punic base at Drepanum before the enemy was aware that the Roman fleet was back in being. As he manned 123 ships needing 36,000 rowers, the fleet must have been down to two-thirds strength before his reinforcements came.

The plan of Claudius was for the fleet to approach by night and attack the harbour at dawn. The Romans embarked a picked force of marines, and set off in a long column, with Claudius bringing up the rear. Later tradition relates that the omens were bad, and that when Claudius was told the sacred chickens would not eat, he cried "Then let them drink!" and sacriliously flung them into the sea! Infactthe Romans seem to have set off ina highly confident mood, with no premonition of defeat.

The Roman attack achieved complete surprise, but there were two faults. First they were late in arriving, so that the Carthaginians had perhaps half an hour's warning. Second Claudius was at the back of the column, where he could not exercise effective command.

It was a further misfortune for the Romans that the Punic admiral, Adherbal, was able and energetic, and his fleet efficient. Quickly recovering his surprise, he had the alarm sounded, the ships manned

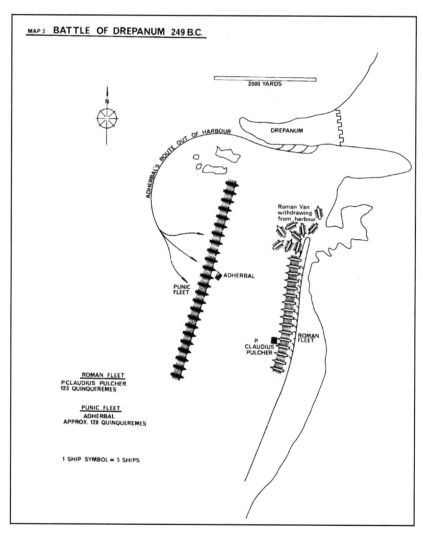

MAP 3 **BATTLE OF DREPANUM** 249 B.C.

2000 YARDS

DREPANUM

ADHERBAL'S ROUTE OUT OF HARBOUR

Roman Van
withdrawing
from harbour

ADHERBAL

PUNIC
FLEET

P
CLAUDIUS
PULCHER

ROMAN
FLEET

ROMAN FLEET
P CLAUDIUS PULCHER
123 QUINQUEREMES

PUNIC FLEET
ADHERBAL
APPROX. 120 QUINQUEREMES

1 SHIP SYMBOL = 5 SHIPS

and led the first five out of the harbour, giving orders for the rest to follow. The Romans were approaching from the south; he hed his ships westwards to the open sea.

The leading Roman ships were now in the harbour area, but seeing all surprise lost and the enemy ships putting to sea, began to retire. Perhaps if Claudius had been up withte van he might still have been able to attack the enemy while they were in confusion, but the opportunity passed.

Adherbal and his five ships, having gained sea room, stopped and formed line abreast, and the rest of the fleet as they came up were ordered to conform. Maenwhile Claudius was also forming line with hisback to the shore; his right wing was in chaos with the ships returning from the harbour in confusion and colliding with one another.

When Adherbal was ready, he gave the signal to engage. The Carthaginian fleet moved in to the attack, and were met by the Romans. At first the battle was evenly contested, because of the superiority of the Roamn marines; then the Punic position, with sea room for their manouevre tactics, started to tell. Of the Roman vessels, 93 were taken by the enemy, and only 30 from the left wing, including that of Claudius himself, escaped back to Lilybaeum.

The battle illustrates how an admiral in antiquity had to overcome limitations in signalling his intentions. Adherbal gave only two signals after the line was formed, "Advance" and "Engage the enemy". His order on leaving harbour was simply "Follow me". The order to form line (and probably information on signals) had to be passed by wordof mouth to the ships as they came up, by staff officers in small boats. Once the "attack" and "engage" signals had been given, there was little that Adherbal could do to influence the course of the battle apart from personal example and orders passed by hailing to nearby vessels.

Following the battle Adherbal returned to Carthage, but his colleague Carthalo, who arrived to take over from him followed up the advantage gained in the battle by raiding the remains of the Roman fleet at Lilybaeum with 100 ships. This time, in contrast to Claudius' raid, things were done properly. The Punic vessels attacked at first light and achieved complete surprise, combined with a sortie from the defenders of Lilybaeum.

Having taken or destroyed a number of ships, Carthalo next moved to oppose Roman reinforcements expected from Syracuse. The Roman ships were moving in two bodies, and Carthalo succeeded in positioning himself between the two, neither of which was prepared to engage him. And here again the superior seamanship of the Carthaginians assisted them, for Carthalo's captains were able to give him warning of an imminent storm, so that he took shelter, and the Romans, caught against the exposed coastline again, lost both fleets.

After the disasterous events of the year 249, the Romans conceded command of the sea to the Carthaginians, and a protracted and inconclusive land campaign dragged on, with the Punic forces skilfully commanded by Hamilcar Barca, the father of the great Hannibal.

In 243 BC the Romans however decided upon a final trial of strength by sea, and a new fleet of 200 vessels was prepared. These ships were commanded by the Consul for 242, Q. Lutatius Catulus, and at the beginning of that year set out for Sicily. The vessels were all of a new design for the Romans, being based upon a very fast Carthaginian vessel captured at the siege of Lilybaeum eight years earlier, and Catulus' tactics were quite different from the usual Roman boarding tactics. Instead it was his aim to beat the Carthaginians by superior seamanship if possible.

Catulus achieved strategic surprise, seizing the harbour at Drepanum and the anchorages at Lilybaeum, and began to lay siege to Drepanum, knowing that the Carthaginians were bound to react.

The Carthaginian fleet had been laid up in the absence of Roman opposition, and was at its home base, but on the news of Catulus' success, was prepared to go to sea and loaded with stores for the campaign. The Carthaginian Admiral, Hanno, could not sail directly for Sicily and risk meeting the Romans at sea while his ships were laden with supplies, and he therefore headed for the most western of the Aegatian islands, Hiera or Holy Island.

The plan was to avoid action with the Romans and reach the coast of Sicily, contact the Carthaginian army under Hamilcar, discharge the supplies, and after embarking soldiers to act as marines, seek out Catulus.

Catulus had no intention of permitting this to happen, and himself embarking his marines, took position on the island of Aegusa. His fleet was well exercised and trained, and in a state of efficiency far above that of any previous Roman force.

The day of the battle dawned with a brisk westerly breeze, and the Carthaginians put to sea, doubtless planning to run in to Sicily with the wind behind them, as earlier in the siege of Lilybaeum, and not expecting the Romans to engage in the rough sea. And indeed Catulus hesitated before boldly ordering the fleet to intercept.

The well trained Romans formed up in single line abreast, despite the weather, and the Carthaginians lowered their masts and sails, and moved to oppose them. The Carthaginians, out of training, manouevre hampered by the stores on board, as well as the main masts and sails, and lacking the picked marines from Hamilcar's army, were no match for the skilled Romans, and the fleet of Catulus sunk 50 ships and took another 70 before the remainder took to flight, hoisting sail, and

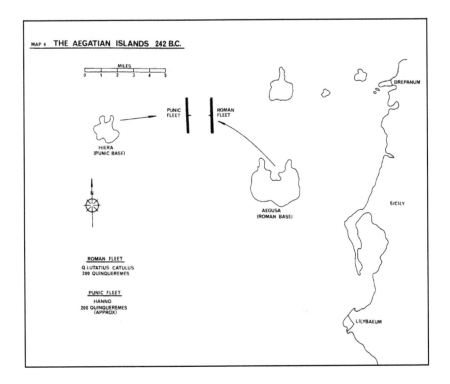

MAP 4 THE AEGATIAN ISLANDS 242 B.C.

MILES
0 1 2 3 4 5

PUNIC FLEET

ROMAN FLEET

DREPANUM

HIERA
(PUNIC BASE)

AEGUSA
(ROMAN BASE)

SICILY

ROMAN FLEET
Q.LUTATIUS CATULUS
200 QUINQUEREMES

PUNIC FLEET
HANNO
200 QUINQUEREMES
(APPROX)

LILYBAEUM

escaping back to Holy Island. Fortunately the wind had now shifted round to the east.

After this battle the Carthaginians conceded the command of the sea to the Romans, and seeing no prospect of successfully prosecuting the war, made peace. The Roman command of the sea was never again challenged by Carthage, although the Roman fleet was not kept in being and was allowed to decline. The knowledge that Rome could if necessary construct a superior fleet remained sufficient deterrent, even though the second Punic War, when Hannibal required reinforcement in Italy.

MACEDON, RHODES & PERGAMUM

At the end of the 3rd Century BC, King Philip V of Macedon was attempting to extend his influence over the Aegean, and in so doing encountered resistance from Rhodes and Pergamum, the naval and commercial powers most affected by his ambitions. In 201 BC there was a war in the Aegean which resulted in a check to Philip's plans, and the main battle was the battle of Chios, in which his fleet was defeated.

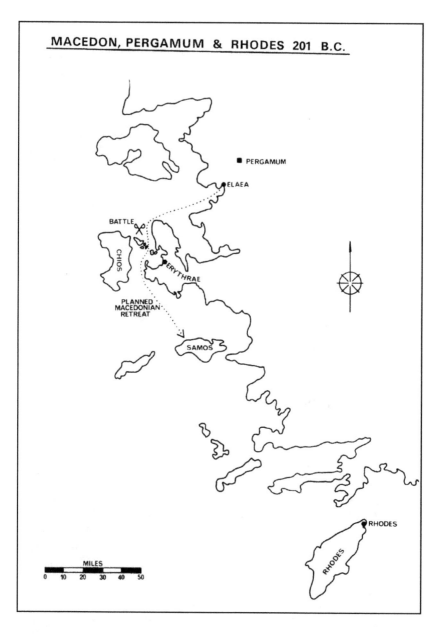

MACEDON, PERGAMUM & RHODES 201 B.C.

PERGAMUM

ELAEA

BATTLE

CHIOS

ERYTHRAE

PLANNED
MACEDONIAN
RETREAT

SAMOS

RHODES

RHODES

MILES

0   10   20   30   40   50

This fleet was a new acquisition, obtained largely from maritime cities
subject to him, and consisted of about 50 cataphract ships, of all types
up to and including a dekares. This was less than the combined fleets
of Rhodes and Pergamum, and to make up his numbers. Philip added
large quantities of lembi - light open boats with perhaps 15 oars per
side to the fleet. Such vessels were always present in small numbers to
act as messengers and scouts with fleets; Philip's idea was for them to
have a fighting role as well.

As far as size of ships was concerned, the Macedonians built large. This was evidently a matter of policy, as Rhodes certainly and Pergamum probably did not have anything larger than a Quinquereme and relied on manouevre tactics. The bigger Macedonian vessels enabled quantities of marines from the unrivalled Macedonian land forces to be carried.

The actual course of events leading up to the battle was simple. Philip advanced his fleet and seized Chios and Samos, and then took Elaea as a base for his army to lay siege to Pergamum itself. His base at Elaea was covered by the allied navies from a point nearby.

Poor progress was made with the siege, and Philip determined to withdraw to Samos. To do so meant running the gauntlet of the superior allied navies, and Philip decided to try to achieve surprise so as to escape without a battle. He accordingly manned his ships without warning and set off suddenly southwards from Elaea.

The allies hastily manned their ships and set off in pursuit. The Pergamene fleet, under King Attalus himself, had either been nearer or was more alert, as it got away first. The Rhodians were later, but their superior ships and crews enabled them to shorten the gap. By the time that the Macedonians reached the strait between Chios and the mainland, therefore, the Pergamene fleet was advancing parallel with the Macedonian ships, and to the east of them, while the leading Rhodian ships were beginning to fall on the slowest Macedonians. Philip had failed to get away, and a battle was inevitable. He therefore led his van in a 90° turn to port, so that his whole fleet formed a battle line on an approximately east-west line, facing north. The allied squadrons then formed line facing Philip; probably there was a fairly long pause while the lines were formed, partly to rest the rowers after the chase, partly because the allies had not pressed the pursuit in formation, but as a general chase.

The fleets involved were, it will be noted, much smaller and more heterogenous than the Roman and Carthaginian fleets which had fought 50 years earlier in the west, both of which were almost exclusively quinqueremes. In the ensuing battle, it is also clear that the Greek seamen of the period were more inventive than their western counterparts as far as tactics were concerned.

The actual battle was really two separate actions, with the Macedonian left and right facing the Rhodians and King Attalus respectively, while Philip himself with a small reserve squadron positioned himself in the rear of his line, near the Onussae islands.

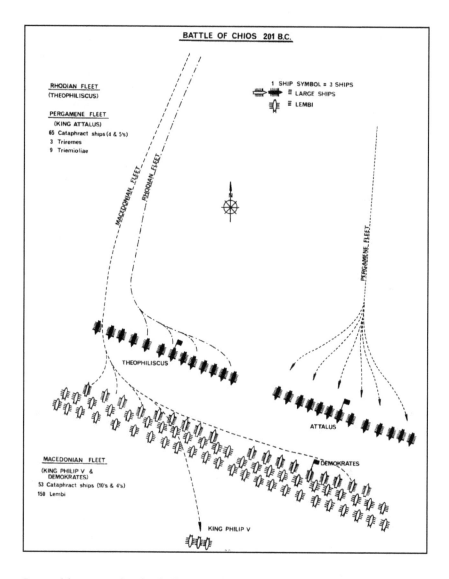

BATTLE OF CHIOS 201 B.C.

RHODIAN FLEET
(THEOPHILISCUS)

PERGAMENE FLEET
(KING ATTALUS)
65 Cataphract ships (4 & 5's)
3 Triremes
9 Triemioliae

1 SHIP SYMBOL = 3 SHIPS
= LARGE SHIPS
= LEMBI

MACEDONIAN FLEET

RHODIAN FLEET

PERGAMENE FLEET

THEOPHILISCUS

ATTALUS

DEMOKRATES

MACEDONIAN FLEET
(KING PHILIP V &
DEMOKRATES)
53 Cataphract ships (10's & 4's)
150 Lembi

KING PHILIP V

It would appear that both fleets had their cataphract ships in single line; the lembi on the Macedonian side supported their big ships to guard against the diekplus tactics which the Rhodians in particular could be expected to adopt.

On the Macedonian right, Philip's flagship, in which was his admiral (Nauarch) Demokrates, was sunk almost immediately; it rammed a triemiolia, one of the weakest enemy vessels present, and its ram became jammed under the main timber supporting the thranite oars, in other words the outrigger. While immobile it was rammed by two triremes from opposite sides, and sank with most of its crew. King Attalus however, had better success, sinking an Octores and then ramming, boarding, and taking another Octores. Another Pergamene vessel had already rammed this second Octores and was stuck just as Philip's flag had been, but the impact of Attalus' ram jarred it clear. The Pergamene fleet gradually got the upper hand in this engagement, which seems to have been an open battle. The Macedonians wherever possible tried to make further ground towards the south, and this action gradually drifted some way apart from the Rhodians. Finally both sides became dispersed as the Macedonians fled.

At this point Attalus himself ran into trouble. Attempting to aid one of his own ships in difficulties, he became separated from his fleet, and was attacked by Philip with his reserve squadron. Attalus was forced to flee eastwards to the mainland, where he abandoned his flagship and scrambled ashore. He got away, having cunningly spread his treasure on the ships deck, so that the pursuers stopped to loot it.

The Rhodians on the other wing also gained the upper hand, although the lembi considerably hampered their manouevre tactics in some parts of the line. From the description given by Polybius, it would appear that this was chiefly round the flagship (a Five) which was supported by other Fives. Since no big Macedonian ships are mentioned on this wing by Polybius, it is probable that they were all on the other wing facing the Pergamene fleet, and the Rhodians were not outclassed as far as size of ship was concerned. At any rate, in the centre they were even engaging in bow to bow ramming, and using a special technique whereby their own bows were depressed, giving an underwater blow, whereas the enemy ram hit above the waterline. This can only have been by some temporary trimming, corrected immediately after the ram, so that the bow again returned to its normal level. As moving all the marines of a Roman Quinquereme of the same period to the stern was sufficient to bring the bows out of the water, it was probably achieved by moving crew forward and dispersing them again immediately after the ram.

In the centre of this action, therefore, a melee took place in which the Rhodian admiral was mortally wounded. The flanks of the Macedonian line were open however, since the battle was so spread out, and here the Rhodians had plenty of water to manouevre. In circumstances like this the many Macedonian lembi were powerless, and no less than 40 of them were sunk by the Rhodians, together with 10 of the cataphract ships on that wing - this means each Rhodian ship sunk two enemy: an astonishing average.

According to the account of Polybius, the Pergamenes on the other wing sank 14 cataphract ships, including the flagship Ten, a Nine, a Seven and a Six; the Macedonians also lost 3 triemioliae here and 25 lembi. Not mentioned in this victory total are the two Eights which were taken and sunk in the battle by King Attalus, unless they are included in the other cataphract ships, unspecified.

Philip had thus lost 26 out of 53 cataphract ships and 72 out of 150 lembi, almost 50%. He nevertheless claimed the victory, partly because he had taken King Attalus' flagship, partly because he happened to pick up most of the bodies. The Allies lost a total 6 ships sunk (3 Rhodian and 3 Pergamene) and 3 Pergamene vessels were captured. The next day the allies formed up in battle line outside Philip's anchorage; the self styled victor did not challenge them.

Although the Battle of Chios resulted in the defeat of the Macedonian navy, it had much more far reaching consequences, for alarm at the challenge which Macedon posed to the existing balance of power in the Aegean prompted the Rhodians to request Roman intervention to redress the balance; the eventual consequences are well known.

THE WAR AGAINST SEXTUS POMPEIUS

Following the assassination of Caesar in 44 BC, his adopted son, Octavian, and chief lieutenant, M. Antonius, waged a successful land campaign against his assassins. The defeat and death of Brutus and Cassius, however, was not the end of the Senatorial power, as their fleet remained in being.

The fleet had been entrusted to the son of Pompeius Magnus, Sextus Pompeius, who had the title of Prefect of the Fleet and the Maritime Shore. Pompeius, following the death of the tyrannicides, still held Sardinia, Corsica, and Sicily, with 9 legions and perhaps 200 ships.

In 40 BC Sextus took advantage of the growing dispute between Octavian and Antony to make trouble, which he did effectively by blocking the grain ships from Egypt, Africa and the West, which supplied Rome. Famine ensued, and in 39 BC Sextus came in splendour with his fleet to Puteoli, and negotiated a settlement with the Triumvirs, confirming and improving his position.

In 38 BC the truce was broken. Pirates, allegedly instigated by Sextus, ravaged the coasts of Italy, and Octavian induced Menodorus, Sextus' governor of Corsica and Sardinia, to change sides and betray the islands to him. Menodorus, a thoroughly unsavoury Greek freedman, complied, and received command of part of Octavian's fleet as a reward. It was a weakness politically of Sextus that he had to officer his fleet with freedmen of this type, efficient as they were as officers.

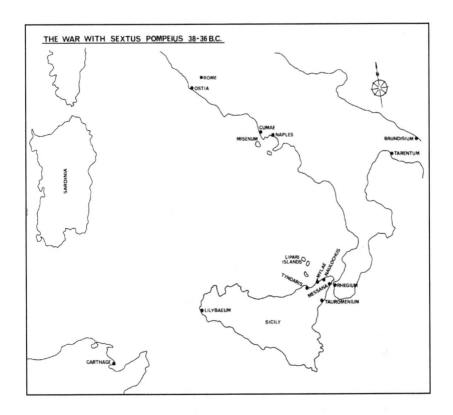

War was now planned in earnest, each side complaining of the bad faith of the other in not keeping the compact of 39 BC Octavian's plan was for two fleets to come down the two sides of Italy and meet at Rhegium, where he was to join them with an army. There the fleet of Sextus would be defeated, the army cross the straits, and overwhelm by sheer numbers the six legions of low grade troops Sextus had (Menodorus had taken 3 with him when he deserted).

The western fleet, under C. Calvisius Sabinus (Consul the year before) and the turncoat Menodorus - an ill assorted pair - was met by Sextus' main fleet. Sextus left only 40 ships at Messana to face the growing power of Octavian across the strait. His main fleet was under the command of another Greek freedman, Menecrates, whose loyalty was assured by his personal hatred of Menodorus. Menecrates may have had over 100 ships.

The Caesarian fleet, perhaps 100 strong, had larger ships than their opponents, but less skilled seamen. When they met Menecrates near Cumae, therefore, they assumed the usual tactics of such a fleet, with backs to the shore. As a variant, however, the line was in a convex form, with both flanks resting on the shore but some clear water behind the centre, giving some room for manouevre and support of threatened parts of the line.

Calvisius himself had some success in the battle, but in general the Pompeians pressed home their attack on the enemy and destroyed and burnt many of them. The highlight of the battle was however the engagement between Menodorus and his rival Menecrates. The rivals saw each other, and abandoning all other thoughts, charged headlong. Menodorus swept away one of Menecrates' oar banks, but lost his own ram in the process, and the two crippled ships ended up side by side. A furious boarding battle ensued, in which Menodorus had the advantage of the larger and higher ship, and Menecrates was mortally wounded, by an iron Spanish javelin.

The result of the battle was thus a victory for the Pompeians, and their new commander, Demochares, retired to Sextus at Messana, while Calvisius set about repairing his fleet. In the meantime Octavian's army and eastern fleet had been facing Sextus small force at Messana without engaging, and the chance of a quick victory over much inferior force was lost when Demochares brought the bulk of the fleet back from Cumae.

Octavian's two fleets were now separated by the enemy, and he moved the eastern fleet north through the straits of Messina to meet Calvisius. While doing so, he was set upon by Sextus, who drove him ashore and destroyed many ships, only breaking off the action when Calvisius was seen approaching from the north. Octavian had thus suffered a defeat, but had unified his two fleets. A further disaster now occurred, with a storm getting up which drove many Caesarian ships on the rocks, but did not harm the Pompeians, who were protected by the harbour of Messina.

This disaster forced Octavian to break off the campaign ignominiously.

In the next year Menodorus changed sides again and returned to Pompeius with seven ships, and Octavian used this as a pretext to dismiss Calvisius and appoint M. Agrippa in his place. Agrippa turned out to be a first class admiral. The year 37 BC he employed in creating a naval base by connecting Lake Avernus, near Naples, to the sea, and in constructing and training crews. In the meantime Octavian obtained a further 120 ships from Antony, in exchange for troops.

The year 36 saw a repetition of the strategic plan for 38, but on a grander scale. On the first day of the month newly named after Julius Caesar, three fleets were to attack Sicily from three different directions.

The third Triumvir, Lepidus, controlled the province of Africa. He had 12 legions, 70 warships, and 1000 transports. Statilius Taurus commanded the ships handed over by Antony (102 only could be manned due to crew losses) at Tarentum. Octavian himself sailed with Agrippa from the new naval base at Puteoli. 21 legions were moved to Southern Italy.

Unfortunately for the masterplan, a southerly gale blew up, so that Lepidus was wafted to Sicily without problem, but Taurus had to put back to Tarentum, and Octavian lost many of his ships wrecked.

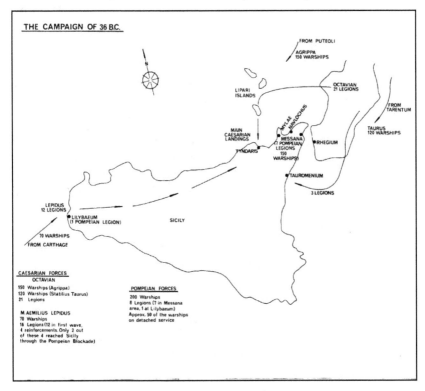

Lepidus got ashore with sufficient force to establish himself in the western half of Sicily, but not enough to clear Sextus from his stronghold about Messana. Sextus was elated by the storm, which he considered a sign of divine protection, and he took the title of Son of Neptune, and started wearing a dark blue Imperator's cloak instead of the usual crimson. His respite was only temporary, however, as Octavian began to rebuild his shattered ships to renew the offensive at the beginning of August.

Perhaps seeing the way the campaign was going, Menodorus, who had been sent to attack the base at Puteoli, which he did with some success, changed sides again; this time however he was given no opportunity for further mischief.

Octavian's renewed campaign started with the seizure by Agrippa of the Lipari islands, which drew the Pompeian fleet to the north coast of Italy, and an inconclusive naval battle took place between the two fleets off Mylae. Thinking that the coast was now clear, Octavian landed a force of troops from Italy at Tauromenium using Statilius Taurus' fleet, but Sextus broke off the action at Mylae and hastened back. Octavian had only got 3 legions ashore when Sextus fell upon Taurus' fleet and defeated it; apparently at least half the ships were lost. The 3 legions left ashore at Tauromenium were therefore cut off.

But in the meantime Agrippa had landed troops who took Tyndaris, and within a few days the legions from Tauromenium succeeded in breaking through to Tyndaris, extricating themselves from a very difficult position by an epic march (in celebration of which their commander thence forward rode home from dinner on an elephant!)

Sextus' fleet apparently needed refitting after the battle off Tauromenium, because it could not effectively oppose Agrippa transferring the main part of Octavian's army from Italy to Tyndaris. Sextus' situation on land was now impossible, but there was one chance left to him. If he could defeat Agrippa's fleet the huge Caesarian army on Sicily would be cut off from supplies, and he could

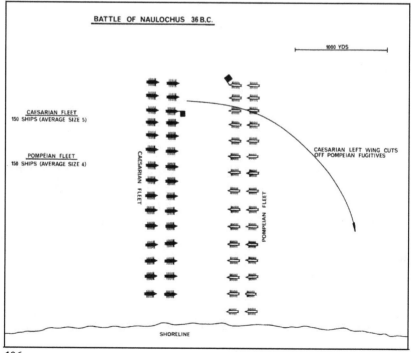

BATTLE OF NAULOCHUS 36 B.C.

1000 YDS

CAESARIAN FLEET
150 SHIPS (AVERAGE SIZE 5)

POMPEIAN FLEET
150 SHIPS (AVERAGE SIZE 4)

CAESARIAN FLEET

POMPEIAN FLEET

CAESARIAN LEFT WING CUTS
OFF POMPEIAN FUGITIVES

SHORELINE

hope for reasonable terms. He therefore staked everything on a naval battle off Naulochus, and issued a challenge to Octavian, which was accepted.

For this final battle at the end of August, both sides had about 150 ships.

In earlier engagements the Pompeians had had a decided advantage in manouevre, and their fleet was probably mainly quadriremes. Sextus own flagship was a 6. The Caesarian fleet was probably mainly quinqueremes. Both fleets were equipped with towers at the bow and stern of the ship, and the only apparent difference between the two fleets was the colour of these towers.

This was apparently an effort by Sextus to nulify Agrippa's earlier boarding advantage.

To nullify the Pompeian manouevre advantage, Agrippa had a tactical surprise in the form of the Harpax. This was a grapnel fired from a dart thrower, which could seize an enemy at a distance. The use of the Harpax ensured that the battle was settled by boarding, and the Caesarian marines were far superior to the troops available to Sextus. At length the surviving Pompeians jettisoned their towers and fled, but only 17 escaped, and it appears that Agrippa's left wing swung round and trapped the rest against the shore.

The campaign was over. Sextus took his surviving 17 ships and fled to Antony, and his land forces surrendered to Lepidus.

Lepidus was now in control of 22 legions, superior force to Octavian, and immediately attempted to take advantage of this situation. Unfortunately he found that his troops would not follow him, and as a result Octavian was left the master of over 40 legions, and the entire western part of the Empire. Lepidus was retired to private life.

Sextus on reaching the east pretended to submit to Antony, but being detected treasonably corresponding with the Parthians, was captured and executed.

THE CAMPAIGN OF ACTIUM 31 B.C.

The final naval war of Octavian resulting in the defeat of M. Antony is difficult to unravel, because all the accounts are more or less propaganda by the victorious side. It seems clear enough however that the strategy of the campaign was decided by Antony, and that he badly under estimated his enemy.

As far as Antony was concerned, Octavian was a young man of little talent, who owed his position entirely to his adoption by Julius Caesar.

Where the two had fought together (at Philippi) the victory had gone to Antony, while Octavian had fled with ignominy. The later campaigns of Octavian, and in particular his naval campaigns, had been attended by terrible disasters, particularly where Octavian personally had been concerned, and the final defeat of Sextus Pompeius had only been accomplished with the aid of ships lent by Antony.

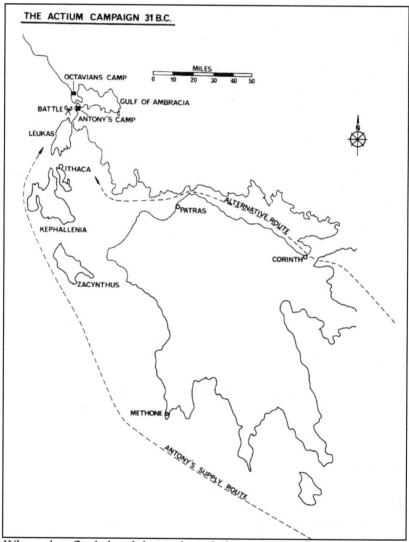

THE ACTIUM CAMPAIGN 31 B.C.

When the final breakdown in relations came, therefore, Antony determined to make his main effort at sea. It was politically essential allied as he was with Cleopatra for him to remain on the defensive, and not invade Italy. To fight on land, as Brutus and Cassius had done, was to face an opponent with better troops, through unrestricted access to the Italian recruiting grounds.

Antony therefore brought his fleet and army to the west coast of Greece. Here his enemy would have to cross the Adriatic with an inferior fleet, and would be very soon brought to a critical condition by lack of supplies, while Antony's own forces, supplied by corn ships from Egypt, suffered no such lack. Antony had 19 legions, and his fleet was probably 8 squadrons of 60 heavy ships, each with 5 scouts, making 520 vessels in total. The main battleships ranged from quadriremes to dekares.

The supply route ran past fortified bases at Methone and Cape Tanaerum: Patras and Corinth were also garrisoned.

Because of Antony's difficulty in getting his fleet manned in the Spring of 31 BC (sickness struck his crews during the winter), Octavian crossed the Adriatic without incident. Before he did, however, Agrippa, in command of his fleet, raided and seized Methone, effectively cutting the main supply route for Antony, and forcing his ships to tranship their cargoes at Corinth instead. Amid the confusion so caused, Octavian moved to a position at the north side of the Gulf of Ambracia.

Here Antony came to take position opposite, on the south side of the Gulf, and here the two forces faced each other for several months. Antony's supply position grew steadily worse, as Agrippa seized Patras and Corinth, forcing Antony to bring all his supplies over the mountains by land. An attempt by Antony's admiral, C. Sosius, to break the blockade failed, and land operations against the Caesarian position were equally unsuccessful. The Caesarian ships were lighter than Antony's, and faster, making them far superior in a war against supply routes.

By August, Antony's prominent supporters were beginning to change sides, and action was imperative.

The plan adopted by Antony cannot now be certainly reconstructed. The ships certainly put to sea with the main masts and sails aboard, which suggests that a breakout was planned, but it would be surprising if Antony should try to break out without at least some attempt to attack the enemy, if only to save face. It is significant, however, that Cleopatra's squadron (in reserve) had the pay chest aboard.

The surviving units of Antony's fleet put to sea, and formed line facing south west, with the Caesarian fleet facing them. There was heavy fighting at the northern most point of the respective lines, where Agrippa and Antony themselves met, and the Caesarian fleet was reversing the tactics which it had used at Naulochus, aiming to cripple the heavier Antonian vessels by manouevre and also by the use of fire (combustibles in earthenware pots fired from engines). Elsewhere the fighting was not nearly so intense, and possibly Antony's left never went into action.

A major factor was the weather; in this area the afternoon the wind normally blows from the north west. When this occurred, Cleopatra's squadron hoisted sail and made off to the southwards, and Antony abandoned his flagship and escaped in a supporting vessel with about 40 other ships. About 100 Antonian vessels therefore in total escaped; the rest either surrendered or returned to harbour.

The surviving Antonian vessels and the army were now in a hopeless position and surrendered on terms within a few days; there was now no effective opposition which Antony could put up to Octavian.

OARS VERSUS SAIL: VENETI, CANNENEFATES & BATAVI

The Roman fleets in the Atlantic, Channel and North Sea met enemies who did not use similar vessels and tactics to their own, as had been the case in the Mediterranean. The normal ship in northern waters was a sailing vessel, stoutly built, not the long light galley.

When therefore Roman ships met an enemy on the sea in such ships, they were at a loss. Normal ram tactics were useless, since the enemy was too stoutly built and damage was likely to be confined to the rammer; equally boarding tactics were difficult because the enemy ships were often higher than the Romans. Most important perhaps was that oared and sailing ships had quite different performance characteristics, so that even to force an engagement was difficult.

The Romans in two particular wars had to contend with this problem. In 56 BC Caesar was faced with the problem of subduing the Gallic tribe of the Veneti, a sea people whose home was in southern Brittany, and in 70 AD during the confusion following the death of Nero, the Romans had to face a revolt on the North Sea coast led by the Batavi and the Canninefates, during which the latter tribe inflicted a serious defeat on the Classis Britannica.

In Caesar's campaign, he found that only in a naval engagement could the Veneti be defeated. Their forts were generally on promontaries and similar places difficult of access from the land, and when the Roman engineers with great exertion constructed moles cutting off such a strong point from the sea, the inhabitants simply took to their ships and moved on.

Caesar accordingly prepared a fleet of standard Mediterranean type. The galleys were probably fairly small, but were fitted with towers, and the main weapon was, as usual with Roman fleets, a powerful force of legionaries on deck; it may be noted that individual ships were under the command of tribunes or centurions. To enable the Romans to board, they were equipped with sharp hooked blades on long poles, to cut the enemy rigging.

The Veneti were able to put 220 ships to sea to oppose the Romans; the ships were tall enough, particularly at the stern, for the crew to overlook the towers on the Roman ships. The Romans nevertheless were able to cut the rigging of certain ships, and then go alongside with

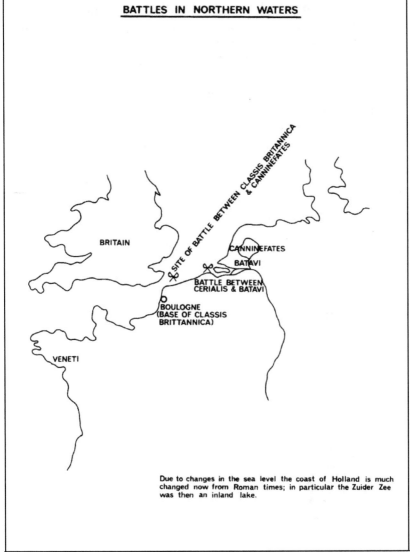

BATTLES IN NORTHERN WATERS

BRITAIN

SITE OF BATTLE BETWEEN CLASSIS BRITANNICA & CANNINEFATES

CANNINEFATES

BATAVI

BATTLE BETWEEN CERIALIS & BATAVI

BOULOGNE (BASE OF CLASSIS BRITTANNICA)

VENETI

Due to changes in the sea level the coast of Holland is much changed now from Roman times; in particular the Zuider Zee was then an inland lake.

several ships at once, letting perhaps 200 legionaries take on the 50 or 60 fighting men in each of the Veneti ships. This tactic would have been of limited service only however if a calm had not providently arisen shortly after the battle started, and it was this rather than the rigging cutters that enabled Caesar to take the majority of the enemy, and destroy the power of the Veneti. It is clear that if the wind had continued, most of the Veneti would have got away from the battle.

Caesar therefore owed his success to a Roman Calm (the opposite perhaps of a Protestant Wind). In the Batavian revolt the Romans had no such naval success.

The revolt was engineered by a Batavian Prince, Civilis, who had been an officer of Roman auxilia, and is described by Tacitus patronisingly as unusually intelligent for a barbarian. Involving not only the Batavi, but also their cousins the Canninefates and the Frisians, he created an uprising. Since the best Roman troops were involved in civil war, and since Civilis for a time pretended to be fighting for Vespasian, the successful contender, all began well. Roman troops were defeated and 24 ships of the Rhine flotilla were captured through the treachery of their Batavian rowers. Early in 70 AD Civilis was in control of the lower Rhine, had defeated the Roman troops in the area, and was being supported by both Gallic and German tribes.

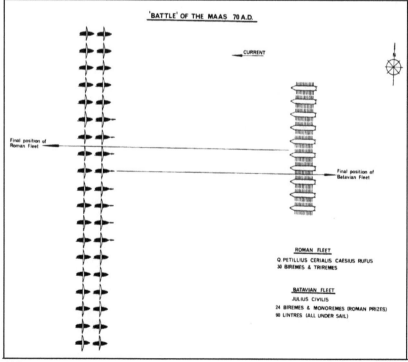

Vespasian had now taken up the purple, and action was in hand to defeat Civilis. The general sent to clear the Rhine was Petilius Cerialis, who had earlier been heavily defeated by Boadicea, but was related to Vespasian, and was therefore of secure loyalty to the new Emperor.

Throughout the campaign that followed, the Batavian ships were boldly handled, and it is clear that Cerialis and the other Roman commanders quite under estimated what the Batavi and their allies were capable of doing.

Cerialis was accompanied on the Rhine by a fleet of triremes and smaller craft; in the course of operations he was ambushed by night by Civilis German allies, who succeeded in towing away several vessels, including Cerialis' own flagship. The General himself was in the embarrassing situation, when this occurred, of being ashore with his mistress, and the sentries claimed they had not given the alarm because Cerialis' orders were that he was on no account to be disturbed!

More serious than this action was a naval battle fought in the North Sea. Legio XIV from Britain had been conveyed to north east Gaul by the Classis Britannica. Having landed the legion, the fleet was attacked by the Canninefates, and most of the ships were sunk or captured.

These bare facts are all Tacitus tells us about this naval battle. We do not even know whether the Canninefates were using their own craft, possibly similar to the ships of the Veneti, or whether they were using captured Roman ships. Clearly, however, they were using sail - Civilis modified all his Roman prizes to take sail - and also the Roman ships did not have the usual benefit of first class marines, having just landed the XIV Legion, and had presumably disembarked their own marine contingents previously to permit as many troops as possible to be carried.

This naval battle, however, did little to halt the advance of the legions towards the Batavian territory, and Civilis made one further effort to confirm his command of the sea.

The battle that followed took place in a small lake at the mouth of the Maas; the object of the Batavians was to gain control of the river, which was being used by Roman supply vessels from Gaul. The fleet which Civilis manned was centred round the 24 Roman prizes (biremes and monoremes) which he had taken; these had all been fitted with sails. They were supported by a number of light open boats, similar to lembi.

The Roman fleet was inferior in numbers to Civilis, but had larger ships; there were probably about 30 Roman vessels, of which the largest were triremes.

The action which followed illustrates the problem of trying to engage a fleet of galleys with a fleet of sailing ships. The Romans were facing west, and had the benefit of the current; the Batavi were facing east, and had the westerly wind behind them.

Both fleets advanced, aided respectively by current and wind, and passed through each other, firing missiles as they went. The Romans now found that they had the current to contend with, and the Batavi were now directly downwind of the Romans, so neither side could re-engage!

The failure to force a decisive engagement by the Batavian fleet meant that the Romans could not now be effectively resisted, and Civilis shortly after capitulated. The effective use made during the campaign of their ships by the northern tribes shows, however, that Roman fleets were not invincible, and that they could be defeated by northern enemies using their own types of vessel.

APPENDIX: Naval Wargames Rules for Large-Scale Fleet Actions 1000 BC to 500 AD

by Richard B. Nelson

INTRODUCTION

The story of ancient naval rules is one of continuous development by a number of people in fairly close contact with each other and sharing their thoughts on the subject freely. The first widely used set was produced by Tony Bath of Southampton. This was replaced by a set produced by Richard Nelson and published in a early edition of "Slingshot" (the Journal of the Society of Ancients). Then came Ed Smith's rules. These went into the actions of individual ships in great detail and as a result worked best when each player controlled only a few ships.

It was therefore felt that there was a need for a set of rules suitable for large fleet actions and this set is the result. It derives from the original Nelson rules, with improved movement and combat procedures and a wholly new section on morale and ship and squadron reactions. The player needs the skills of an admiral rather than just those of a captain and will often be in control of a hundred or more ships.

I. SHIP TYPES PERMITTED

These Rules are intended to cover the warfare of the Ancient Seafaring peoples of the Mediterranean during the thousand years from the first recorded engagements of Greeks and Phoenicians to the fall of the Western Roman Empire, and to be especially suitable for large fleet actions.

The Rules cover all types of ship employed by these peoples, with the exception of the very largest polyremes, which were not a practicable fighting proposition. Equally, all types of tactics are covered, although some of the more far fetched expedients (such as slinging vipers in fragile earthenware pots onto an opponents deck) are not directly included.

The various types of vessels covered are detailed in the Table of Factors: the meaning of the various factors will be explained in the appropriate following sections.

The ships in the table are:

1. Open Galleys (rowers at least partially exposed).

Pentekonter, lembi: light open galleys with up to 50 rowers used as despatch boats etc., and also to support heavy ships in battle.

Hemiolia: A light bireme favoured by pirates and designed for use under both oars and sail.

Liburnian: A light bireme, similar in concept to the lembi, originally used by Illyrian pirates, and subsequently used by the Romans.

Trireme: The standard battleship of Classical Greek fleets and their opponents. Light and heavier versions were built by navies with varying tactical ideas.

Triemiolia: A trireme designed to operate under oars and sail as a pirate catcher, devised by the Rhodian navy.

2. Cataphract Galleys (rowers completely enclosed by deck etc.)

Quadrireme: the fastest and smallest of the cataphract ships.

Quinquereme: the standard battleship of the Roman Republic and of Carthage.

Larger Polyremes: these were generally flagships etc., and ranged up to a Forty, but the largest normally used was a Sixteen. Use of these big ships was confined to the Hellenistic Greeks and their allies, except where prizes were used by an enemy.

All cataphract ships could carry towers to give added height to marines, and also carried war engines.

3. Other vessels: These include the merchant ships of the Mediterranean and the sail powered warships of the Veneti

II. SETTING UP THE GAME

1. The playing area consists of a board or table marked either with hexagons or offset rectangles. Each of these spaces holds one ship and the optimum size of space is therefore one which will accommodate one model without overlap or excessive open space surrounding the ship.

2. The addition of terrain; shoreline, small islands or rocks - will improve the game and add to realism since most ancient sea battles were fought near the shore. Where terrain is not set out by mutual agreement between the players it is suggested that each player select terrain and set it out on the table where desired, the amount of terrain being selected by dice.

3. Different types of ship have different points values in the rules and a realistic result is obtained where fleets of equal points value, but different type, are matched. The rules permit ancient battles to be refought with 1 model representing 1 ship.

The actual distance moved by a ship in one period of play is equivalent to that which would have been covered in about 30 seconds. Timescale is therefore as usual with wargame rules somewhat unrealistic.

4. In addition to the ship models and terrain, players will require normal and average dice, and counters of various colours. These latter are placed beside ships to indicate when they are crippled etc. Alternatively where ships of many different types, carrying engines and towers are deployed, it will be more convenient to keep a logsheet showing the various ships and the data pertaining to them. A specimen logsheet is shown on the next page.

5. For typical ancient fleets and for details of the tactics employed by ancient Admirals, the reader is referred to the earlier sections of this book.

A table giving the ship data sheet is shown on the page 119.

SPECIMEN LOGSHEET

SHIP IDENTIFICATION	SHIP TYPE	CREW TYPE	EQUIPMENT — SAILS (MAINSAIL ON BOARD / MAINSAIL UP / BOOMSAIL UP)	ENGINES (FITTED / JETTISONED TRAILED)	IRON HANDS (CORVUS FITTED / OTHER ON HANDS)	TOTAL POINTS COST	M.F.s FATIGUE POINT	USED UNDER OAR (UNSKILLED CREW / TRAINED CREW / SKILLED CREW)	CURRENT STATUS
① CONCORDIA	SIX	TRAINED		✓	✓	85			
② SABRINA	HEAVY QUINQ	"	✓	✓	✓	65			CRIPPLED 11 BF RECOVERED 1
③ TANAIS	"	"	✓	✓	✓	65			SUNK
④ SEQUANA	LT TRIREME	SKILLED	✓ ✓			40			
⑤ NAIAS	HEMIOLIA	TRAINED	✓ ✓			35			
⑥ DRYAS	HEMIOLIA	TRAINED				35			

RECOMMENDED THAT SHIP MODELS BEAR A SMALL NUMBER ON DECK FOR EASY IDENTIFICATION OR BE COLOUR CODED

N.B. THE SHIPS YET HAVE NONE OF THE CREW TIRED

SHIP DATA SHEET

SHIP TYPE	Untrained crew — Cost Points	Move Factor	Factor to Pivot	Trained crew — Cost Points	Move Factor	Factor to Pivot	Skilled Crew — Cost Points	Move Factor	Factor to Pivot	Ram Factor	Boarding Factor	Towers — Cost Points	Add to BF	Engines — Cost Points	BF Effect	Iron Hands — Cost Points	Add to BF
Pentekonter/Lembi	10	3	1	15	3	½	20	4	½	1	1	—	—	—	—	—	—
Hemiolia	15	4	1	20	4	½	25	5	½	1	1	—	—	—	—	—	—
Liburnian	15	4	1	20	4	½	25	5	½	1	1	—	—	—	—	—	—
Triemiolia	30	5	2	35	5	1	45	6	1	1	2	—	—	—	—	—	—
Light Trireme	25	5	2	30	5	1	40	6	1	1	1	—	—	—	—	5	1
Heavy Trireme	25	5	2	30	4	1	40	5	1	2	2	—	—	—	—	5	1
Light Quadrireme	30	5	2	35	5	1	45	6	1	2	2	—	—	—	—	5	1
Heavy Quadrireme	35	4	2	40	4	1	50	5	1	3	4	5	1	5	1	5	1
Light Quinquereme	40	4	2	45	4	2	55	5	1	3	3	—	—	—	—	5	1
Heavy Quinquereme	45	4	3	50	4	2	60	4	1	2	5	5	1	5	1	5	1
'Six'	50	4	3	60	4	2	75	4	2	3	6	10	2	10	2	5	1
'Seven'	60	4	3	70	4	2	85	4	2	4	7	10	2	10	2	5	1
'Eight'	70	4	3	80	4	2	95	4	2	4	8	10	2	10	2	5	1
'Nine'	80	4	3	90	4	2	105	4	2	4	9	10	2	10	2	5	1
'Ten'	90	4	3	100	4	3	115	4	2	5	10	10	2	10	2	5	1
'Eleven'	100	4	4	110	4	3	125	4	3	5	11	15	3	15	3	5	1
'Twelve'	110	4	4	120	4	3	135	4	3	5	12	15	3	15	3	5	1
'Thirteen'	120	4	4	130	4	3	145	4	3	5	13	15	3	15	3	5	1
'Fourteen'	130	4	4	140	4	3	155	4	3	5	14	15	3	15	3	5	1
'Fifteen'	140	4	4	150	4	3	165	4	3	5	15	15	3	15	3	5	1
'Sixteen'	150	4	4	160	4	3	175	4	3	5	16	—	—	—	—	—	—
Merchant Ship	15	2	1	15	2	1	20	3	1	0/5	0	—	—	—	—	—	—
Armed Sailing Ship	25	2	1	25	2	1	30	3	1	0/5	10	—	—	—	—	5	1
Saxon Ship	—	—	—	20	4	1	—	—	—	0/1	1	—	—	—	—	—	—

Sailing Ship RF (e.g. 0/5): 0 = RF when ramming.
5 = RF when rammed.

119

III. SYNOPSIS OF PERIOD:

1.   Determine Weather if required.

2.   Determine Reactions from previous period and any optional Reactions.

3.   Cripples throw dice.

4.   Player A moves ships.

5.   Player B moves ships.

6.   Determine results of ramming.

7.   Determine boarding actions.

IV. WEATHER

1. At the start of the battle the Weather conditions are determined. Two dice are thrown, 1 normal, 1 average. The normal dice determines wind direction, as illustrated: note that the wind always blows at right angles to two opposing hexagon sides.

The average dice (233445) determines wind strength:

2	Calm.
3 or 4	Light Breeze, Calm Sea.
5	Strong Breeze, Rough Sea.

2. These weather conditions will remain constant unless either player seeks a change in the weather. To do this, in any period, before the ships are moved, either player may throw one average dice for wind direction and/or one for wind strength. Dice may be thrown only once per period for weather.

In all cases 3s and 4s mean no change.

On the Wind Direction Dice
2 means that the wind shifts 60° clockwise,
5 60° anticlockwise;

A 5 has been thrown so the wind blows
in the direction of the arrow.

On the Wind Strength Dice
2   means that the weather improves
        (i.e. Strong Breeze becomes Light Breeze),
5   that it worsens.

3. If there is a Strong Breeze/Rough Sea and the weather worsens, a storm is imminent. Neither player may try to change the weather for 6 periods.

At the end of 3 periods any vessel not in Shelter and with an unskilled crew must turn head to wind and throw 1 dice per period. Ships with trained crews turn to wind after 4 periods, and ships with skilled crews after 5 periods.

Results of the dice throws are as follows:
1   vessel is swamped and sunk.
2, 3   vessel drifts I space downwind.
4 - 6   vessel maintains position.

Ships drifting ashore are deemed wrecked, and ships drifting off the table are deemed swamped and lost.

Shelter consists of:
Any space in the lee of an island, headland or reef,
or drawn up on any beach,
or off the table over own baseline or windward baseline.

Ships with skilled crews add 1 to their dice throws in a Storm;

Ships with unskilled crews deduct 1.

4. All weather changes take place immediately except Storms. See Synopsis of period.

An example of a storm is shown on the next page.

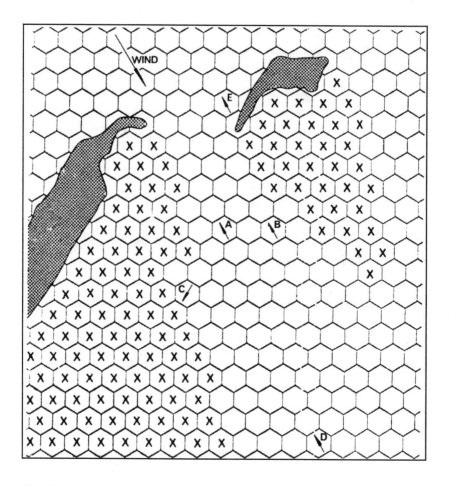

ILLUSTRATION OF STORM:

Spaces with a cross are in the Lee of the headland and island. It is the 5th period after the storm became imminent.

Ship A (unskilled crew) throws a 2. -1 (unskilled crew) means that the ship is swamped, as it brings the dice back to 1.

Ship B (trained crew) throws a 4, and does not move.

Ship C (skilled crew) is not affected by the storm until the end of the 5th period, so need not throw and can move into the lee of the headland.

Ship D (trained crew) throws a 3, so drifts 1 space downwind. This takes the ship off the table so it is deemed lost.

Ship E (trained crew) also throws a 3, so drifts onto the island and is wrecked.

V. MOVEMENT UNDER OARS

1. Play takes place on a table or board marked either with a hexagon grid or with offset rectangles. Each ship occupies 1 space, and not more than one ship can occupy a space at any one time. On the hexagon grid ships must always be at right angles to 2 opposing hexagon sides; with offset rectangles ships must always be at an angle of 90° or 30° to the short sides of the rectangle (see illustration).

2. Each vessel has a number of Movement Factors (MF) which are governed by its type and crew, and are detailed on the table of Factors. Each MF may be used once per period to move the ship one space forward or to pivot 600 port or standard. Certain ships pivot faster (using 1 MF) or slower (using 2/3 MF) depending upon type etc.

3. All ships may move 1 space backwards, using 2 MF.

4. When a ship attempts to enter an occupied space, a collision occurs (see RAMMING). The ramming ship puts its bow into the occupied space but itself remains in and subsequently moves from its own space.

5. Opponents move alternatively (see Synopsis of Period).

6. Towing. A ship may tow another. 1 period is required to pass a tow from the bow of one ship to the stern of another (the two ships being in adjacent spaces) and the towed ship then follows the tower in the space behind. The MF of the towing ship is reduced by 1, plus 1 for every difference between the two ships Ram Factors, but always leaving the towing ship 1 MF. (thus a very small ship can still tow a large one at 1 MF per period). To turn under tow, the following procedure must be adopted:

   i)   Towing ship pivots.

   ii)   Tower and towed move forward simultaneously 1 space.

   iii)   Towed ship pivots.

7. Crew Fatigue. MFs under oars are recorded, and when a certain number have been exceeded, the Crew of that ship are tired, and the MF is reduced under oars by 1 MF for each subsequent period. There is also a Reaction penalty.

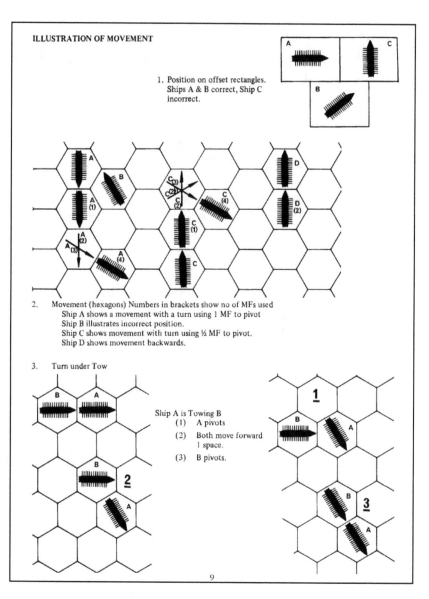

Unskilled Crews tire after 24 MFs under oar
Trained Crews tire after 32 MFs under oar
Skilled Crews tire after 40 MFs under oar

VI. MOVEMENT UNDER SAIL

1. Galleys have two sets of sailing gear available, a Main Sail and a Boat Sail. The Main Sail is normally left ashore, but the Boat Sail is always carried.

2. Ships under MS move at normal MF with the wind on the stern quarter, MF plus I downwind, MF --2 into the wind. The MF is in all cases governed by the ships heading at the start of the period.

3. Ships may not sail directly into the wind or tack across the eye of the wind (i.e. they can wear only). This applies even under oars if the sail is up.

4. Ships may hoist the Boat Sail at any time, taking -1 MF to do so. They then sail as under Main Sail, except that they cannot sail into the wind.

5. It takes 1 period for a ship to raise or lower Main Sail during which the ship can do nothing else.

6. Hemiolia & Triemiolia: These ships, designed to fight under oars and sail, may raise or lower MS at any time using 1 MF. They ignore any Reaction or other penalties for having MS aboard, or being under sail, and other ships ignore Hemiolias and Triemiolias under sail for Reaction purposes.

Illustration of various sail movements.

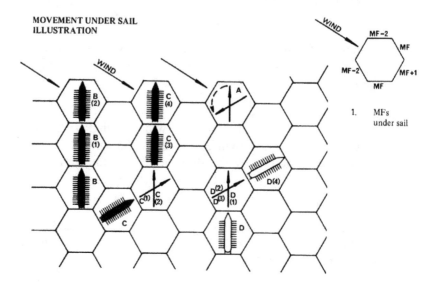

Ship A shows a tack across the eye of the wind – not permitted.

Ship B (MF 4) shows the maximum move into the wind under sail.

Ship C (MF 4) also moves into the wind but has 4MF in the period because of the heading at the start of the period.

Ship D is an hemiola, starting the period under oars, turning, hoisting the sail, and setting off under sail. Total 4 MF used.

The illustration shows two ships, the first facing side A of the hexagon and the second facing side C. Both ship wish to turn to face sides B & D respectively.

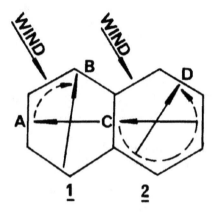

The first ship Tacks. in other words it makes a turn to the right, across the direction from which the wind blows.

The second ship Wears. it turns to the left, presenting its stern to the wind and pivots on round until it faces side D.

Ships under these rules only Wear, not Tack.

VII. RAMMING

1. Ramming results from the collision of vessels, and each ship has a Ram Factor (RF).

2. If 2 ships meet bow to bow, a vessel with a lower RF is Crippled; if the RF is 2 lower than the opponent, it is sunk. If the RF's are equal, each ship throws 1 dice and if the dice is 1-3, the ship throwing is Crippled.

3. If the Rammer rams the opponents Bow Quarter, before contact the target ship may pivot to meet the ram Bow/Bow, provided it is:
   - not crippled.
   - equal in Crew training to the ramming ship.
   - equal in MY to the ramming ship.

If target ship cannot pivot to meet the enemy bow/bow, and its RF is 1 higher or less than rammers RF, it is sunk. If not, each ship throws 1 dice, and a ship with RF plus dice lower than opponent is crippled. If two ships ram a third simultaneously, their RFs are added together, and it is treated as I ram. Simultaneously means in the same period.

Two ships or more may threaten to ram, and the target ship must indicate when the nearest is 2 spaces away which threat it will pivot to meet (if permitted). Enemy may then alter course of his vessels.

4. A Ram on the stern quarter may be converted to a ram on the stern under the same circumstances as for a ram on the bow quarter. If the target ship does not pivot, the effect is as for a ram on the bow quarter.

5. If the Rammer rams the stern, ships with RF up to 1 higher than rammer are crippled. Ships with RF2 lower are sunk.

6. If ships come into contact and neither strikes with its ram (e.g. if one drifts into another) both are crippled.

7. A ram normally terminates a ships move. However ships with skilled crews may elect to Cripple instead of Sink (except on a bow/bow ram), in which case 1 MF is used for the Ram, and the ship continues.

8. Where the ram terminates the move, the ramming ship must back water before turning and moving off, and must throw 1 dice at the beginning of the period to see if it succeeds in extricating the ram. A throw of 3-6 means successful withdrawal; skilled crews add 1 to the dice, unskilled subtract 1.

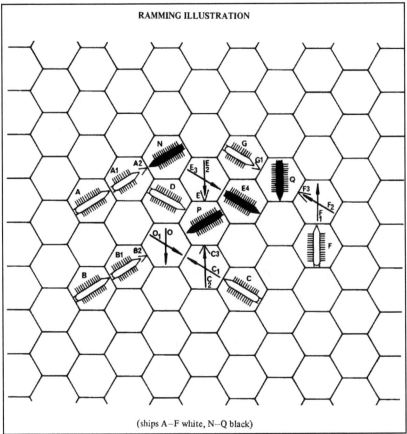

RAMMING ILLUSTRATION

(ships A–F white, N–Q black)

See the diagram above:

Ship A takes 2 MF and rams Ship N bow/bow. Both throw 1 dice. N throws 4, A throws 2. A is Crippled. (A and N have equal RF).

Ships B and C Feint at ship 0, which pivots to face C. Ship B then rams 0 in stern quarter. Bs RF is 2, 0's RF is 3, therefore 0 is sunk.

Ship C having feinted at 0 moves forward and cripples ship P, using 1 MF to do so.

Ship D rammed P last period and now seeks to withdraw. Dice throw is 3 but D's crew is unskilled, bringing the score to 2; so D cannot move.

Ship E is in a similar position to D, but throws 5, so backs water, turns, and moves away. Ships F and G both ram ship Q within the period, i.e. simultaneously.

F's RF is 2, G's RF is 3, Q's RF is 5. Normally neither F or G could sink Q, but by ramming simultaneously the RFs are added making 5; Q is therefore sunk.

VIII. CRIPPLED & SUNK SHIPS

1. A ship which is Sunk remains in position of the table but plays no further part in the game (i.e. it floats waterlogged).

2. A Crippled ship, if stationary when hit, pivots 60° in the direction of the cripple (i.e. if port side is hit, pivot to port); if moving when hit, it moves 1 space forward and then pivots in the direction of the cripple. If both sides are crippled simultaneously then there is no swing, nor is there with a bow/bow or bow/stern ram.

3. A Crippled ship is immobilised after the compulsory swing. It may resist Boarding but the BF is reduced by half. At the beginning of each period 1 dice is thrown, with the following effect:

5 - 6	recovers fully and may move etc. unimpaired immediately.
3 or 4	ship remains immobilised but regains original BF
2	remains immobilised.
1 or less	ship sinks

Deduct 1 from the dice for each of the following:
- untrained crew.
- Rough Weather.
- Corvus, towers, or engines aboard (towers may be jettisoned once original BF is recovered).
- Mainsail aboard (whether up or not).

4. A ship may be Crippled more than once and dice are thrown each period for each cripple, each of which must be separately escaped from before the ship can move.

5. A ship which has recovered original BF may board any ship in contact or hoist the boat Sail

6. If there is a wind, crippled and sunk ships drift I space down wind every period, retaining their original heading.

7. All Crippled ships sink immediately a Storm affects them.

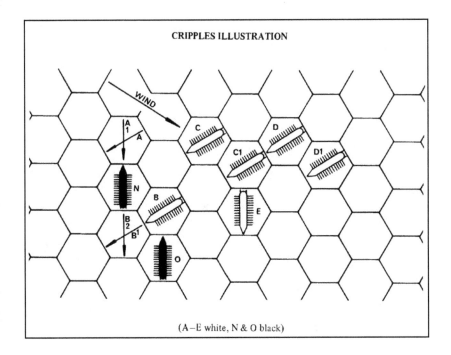

CRIPPLES ILLUSTRATION

(A–E white, N & O black)

Ship A (stationary) is Crippled by ship N and pivots 60° port

Ship B (moving) is Crippled by Ship 0, so moves forward 1 space before pivoting. Ship C is already twice Crippled and throws 2 dice, getting 5 & 1.

Ship C is therefore recovered from one cripple but sunk on the other and drifts downwind 1 space. Ship D is double Crippled and throws 4, recovering the original BF, with 1 dice, but only 2 with the other. D must throw 3 or better in respect of this Cripple before original BF is recovered.

Ship E is double crippled and throws 5,5. It therefore escapes both Cripples and may move unimpaired.

IX. BOARDING AND PRIZES

1. Each vessel has a Boarding Factor (BF) representing the fighting power of the marines on deck.

2. Any vessel in contact with another vessel may board. To determine the result, each slip throws 1 dice and adds this to the BF. If either ship's dice plus BF is 2 higher than the opponent, the opponent is taken; otherwise there is no result.

3. If either side has more than one ship together in contact in one melee with an opponent, all the BFs are added together and 1 dice per side is thrown. The result affects all the ships in that particular melee, all being taken if their dice throw plus combined BFs is lower by 2 than opponents. The two sides may however elect to split up a large melee by mutual agreement. Ships must be in contact with an enemy to take part in a combined melee.

4. A ship with its bows in contact with the enemy, or having just had a higher boarding score than its opponent, may break contact on the next period of movement.

5. A ship once taken is moved by the captor. 2 MF per period only under oars are permitted.

6. A ship can board and retake a prize if its BF plus 1 dice equals or exceeds prizes original BF. The retaken prize assumes former status after one period halted reorganising.

7. Towers: certain ships may be equipped with towers, which add to the BF. See table of factors. Towers may be jettisoned in any period when the ship is not engaged in boarding.

8. War Engines: Certain ships carry war engines if desired. The effect of engines is to reduce the BF of any ship within 3 spaces by the figure given for the type on the Table of Factors (thus a Six with engines can reduce an opponents BF by 2). Engines may only be used on a ship in clear view and cannot be used if the ship firing is engaged in boarding.

9. Iron Hands: This is a generic term for the various types of grappling irons, corvus etc., used by certain fleets. A ship in contact with an opponent equipped with Iron Hands cannot break off unless the opponent permits it. The corvus in addition permits the vessel equipped with it to 'arrest' and board any ship passing through any of the three spaces at the bow. The vessel arrested stops immediately, except that a

vessel coming in to ram the corvus equipped ship will carry out the ram. The corvus can only engage one opponent at a time; other types of Iron Hand can engage any number of opponents at once.

10. Archery: The effect of this is included in the boarding factor, as only when massing to board or to repel boarders is a worthwhile target offered, crew and rowers being largely protected by the ships structure.

Examples of Boarding.

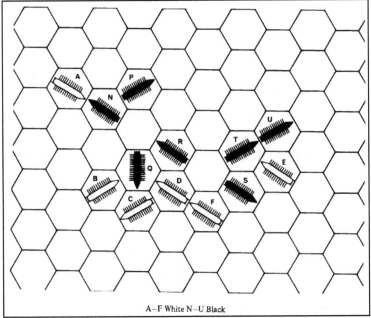

A–F White N–U Black

Ship A (BF 2) is boarded by ship N (BF 3). Each throws 1 dice scoring respectively 6 & 3. A's boarding score is 8, N's is 6, so A takes N. Note that ship P (even if in contact with N) could not intervene in this battle as it is not in contact with an opponent.

Ships B C & D board ships Q & R. BFs are 2, 2,4 and 4,4 respectively and in addition Q & R have towers adding 1 to their BFs. Each side throws 1 dice, white 3, black 4. White BFs total 8 plus 3 on the dice giving 11. Black BFs total 10 plus 4 on the dice making 14. Q & R therefore capture B C & D as their combined BFs plus dice exceeded opponents by 2. This action could have been fought as two melees if the opponents had desired, Q fighting B & C and R fighting D. Note ship F could not intervene in the melee, even if in contact with D, because D & F are on the same side.

Ship E is fitted with corvus and could arrest S T or U and board.

Engines: Ship T if fitted with engines could have fired upon ship D and reduced D's BF accordingly. T could not fire upon F as T does not have a clear view of F.

X FLEET ORGANISATION & REACTION

1. All fleets are split into squadrons led by Commodores, and in addition have a Flagship, leading a Flag Squadron. Flagships and Commodores count as having a crew one degree better than that paid for: i.e. a Commodore with a trained crew is counted as having a skilled crew.

2. The Flagship and the Commodores may not total more than 20% of the whole fleet. There may be less squadrons than Commodores, in which case spare Commodores must be allocated to the Flagship's squadron. Squadrons may be of any size, but must have a commodore.

3. Scouting and despatch boats totalling up to 5% of the fleet are excluded from the squadron organisation.

4. Factors of Morale are determined on a Squadron basis, and each Squadron must take a Reaction test under the following circumstances:
   - On any occasion when any ship of the squadron comes within 5 spaces of an enemy, all the squadron having in the previous period having been more than 5 spaces away from any enemy.
   - When own Squadron becomes `minus' and at each subsequent loss to Squadron.
   - When own Commodore goes `minus'.
   - When an adjacent Squadron becomes `minus'.
   - When the Flagship or Flagship's Squadron becomes `minus'.

5. Definitions of "PLUS & MINUS Ships.

A`PLUS' ship is:	A`MINUS' ship is:
A ship with all factors intact	A crippled ship
A ditto Commodore or Flag	A ship with Tired Crew
(i.e. an intact Commodore or	A captured ship
Flag counts as 2 plusses)	A sunk ship
	A ship with sail hoisted (except hemiolias & triemiolias).
	A ship with towers jettisoned.
	A ship detached from its squadron by more than 3 spaces.

A`PLUS' Squadron is a Squadron with more plusses than minuses. When the minusses exceed the plusses it is a`MINUS' Squadron.

6. To take the Reaction Test, two dice are thrown (average by Sq. with a majority of trained or skilled crews, normal by unskilled Squadrons). The following additions and subtractions are made:

ADD 1 for each	SUBTRACT 1 for each
Plus ship in Squadron	Minus ship in Squadron
Friendly Plus Squadron	Friendly Minus Squadron
Enemy Minus Squadron	Enemy Plus Squadron

Only 1 dice is thrown by a Minus Squadron taking the Test.

If the resulting score is over 6, the Squadron is unaffected.

If the score is over 0, the Squadron must retire to a position more than 5 spaces from any enemy, and not advance closer until a Reaction over 6 is obtained.

If the score is 0 or less, the Squadron must hoist sail and retire from the table. Any ships unable to escape must surrender.

7. Any Squadron may take the Test voluntarily.

Note: A squadron which is Minus can become Plus: e.g. if a number of crippled ships in the Squadron recover.

8. If the Commodore is sunk or captured a substitute must be designated from the squadron survivors. Substitutes do not enjoy higher crew status or count 2 plusses.

9. White Squadron has A (Commodore) crippled, G & H Captured, E sunk, and F detached, and is thus a Minus Squadron.

See an example of a reaction test on the next page.

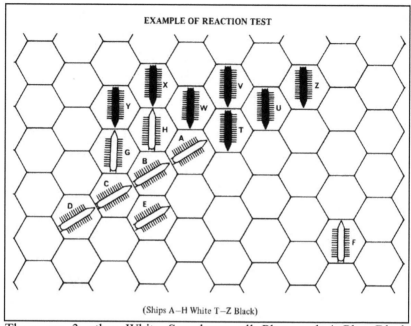

EXAMPLE OF REACTION TEST

(Ships A–H White T–Z Black)

There are 3 other White Squadrons, all Plus, and 4 Plus Black Squadrons, with 1 Black Minus Squadron.

As a Minus Squadron, the White Squadron throws 1 dice, scoring 3. To this are added 3 Plus Ships

(B, C, & D) and 3 Plus Squadrons. From this are subtracted 5 Minus Ships (A, E, F, G & H), and 4 Plus Black Squadrons. Finally 1 Minus Black Squadron is added.

The final total is thus:

dice	3
Plus Ships	3
Plus own Squadrons	3
Minus enemy Squadrons	1
TOTAL	10

less	5
Minus Ships	4
Enemy Plus Squadrons	9

Giving a total of 1, on which the Squadron must retire to a position at least 5 spaces from an enemy and remain there until a better Reaction is obtained. Note that if A recovers from the cripple or F rejoins the Squadron or G or H are recaptured it will no longer be a Minus Squadron.

Printed in the USA
CPSIA information can be obtained
at www.ICGtesting.com
LVHW080423071123
763186LV00005B/362